THE SCANDALMONGER

The Scandalmonger

T. H. WHITE

This edition first published in 2012
by Faber and Faber Ltd
Bloomsbury House, 74–77 Great Russell Street
London WC1B 3DA

Printed by Books on Demand GmbH, Norderstedt

All rights reserved
© Lloyds TSB Offshore Trust Co. Ltd, 1952

The right of T. H. White to be identified
as author of this work has been asserted in accordance
with Section 77 of the Copyright, Designs and Patents Act 1988

This book is sold subject to the condition that it shall not, by way of trade or otherwise, be lent, resold, hired out or otherwise circulated without the publisher's prior consent in any form of binding or cover other than that in which it is published and without a similar condition including this condition being imposed on the subsequent purchaser

A CIP record for this book is available from the British Library

ISBN 978-0-571-29602-6

Our authorised representative in the EU for product safety is
Easy Access System Europe, Mustamäe tee 50, 10621 Tallinn, Estonia
gpsr.requests@easproject.com

CONTENTS

I	RESPECTFUL ATTENTION	9
II	A STRUGGLE OF SENTIMENT	25
III	VARIOUS COMFORTERS	35
IV	OLD SCHWELLY	50
V	DRY BLOOD AND DISTANT THUNDER	58
VI	BACKWATERS	80
VII	ECCENTRICS	91
VIII	AN EARLY SURREALIST	111
IX	A PRIVATE PAESTUM	116
X	FIRE! FIRE!	137
XI	BRIBERY AND CORRUPTION	142
XII	SHERRY	159
XIII	PURE GRIM DEVILS	171
XIV	SCANDAL	175
XV	A TROUBLESOME CARGO — MORE NOISE THAN DANGER	184
XVI	THE BUTTERFLY	192
XVII	THE QUEEN, THE QUEEN!	208
	NOTES ON THE ILLUSTRATIONS	220

ILLUSTRATIONS

BLOODY NEWS	*facing p.* 16
LORD CAMELFORD	32
ILLUSTRATION FROM TYBURN CHRONICLE	64
RURAL SCENE	80
OLD Q ON THE BALCONY	96
CHEVALIER D'EON	97
SCENE IN BEDLAM	112
CHAIRING THE MEMBER	144
UNCORKING OLD SHERRY	160
TALES OF WONDER	172
CI-DEVANT OCCUPATIONS	180
GEORGE BRUMMELL	198

THE SCANDALMONGER

CHAPTER ONE

Respectful Attention

THE Duel was a convention of Latin origin, which came to England late. It had flourished more vigorously in the less phlegmatic soils of France and Italy, and it took root in the hysteria of Ireland in a more widespread and furious manner than it did among the Anglo-Normans.

In the seventeenth century, it was a convention of atrocity. Men had fought like animals, with a weapon in each hand. The seconds were often engaged in the mêlée as well as the principals. All rushed together with little attempt at thrust or parry, and, hugging at close quarters, probed with stiletto and rapier, until the half of them lay dead upon the field. The engagement was like some brawl in the sea-ports of Latin America: ferocious, emotional and without rules. The combatants survived a strange amount of punishment.

In France, for instance, in the reign of Henri IV, two gentlemen called Bazanez and Lagarde Vallon had trouble about a hat.

They set to [says Steinmetz], on the instant. Lagarde came down at once with a vigorous cut on the head of Bazanez, but the frontal bone was so hard that it turned off the weapon. The second cut, however, went in, and Lagarde said, 'That's for the hat.' 'This is for the feather,' he added, with another thrust. 'And this is for the tassel,' a third time he said by way of conclusion. Bazanez lost a great deal of blood, but was not done for yet. He made an extreme effort, rushed upon his opponent, and got him down. In this position he drove his poignard repeatedly in a line between his neck and shoulder, saying, 'I am giving you a scarf to wear with the hat.' He gave him fourteen stabs from the neck to the navel. At each stab Bazanez exclaimed, 'Beg for your life.' 'No, no!' said Lagarde, 'not yet, my dear fellow'; and, hacked about as he was in every part of his body, he bit off the chin of his slaughterer, and smashed the back of his head with the pommel of his sword. This put an end to the conflict.

There can be few English duellists who have bitten off the chins of their opponents — incidentally, both Bazanez and Lagarde survived — but the bestiality of the engagements was scarcely on a higher level in England during the same century. The following was an Earl of Dorset's description of a duel, which he fought in 1613.

I made a thrust at my enemy, but was short; and on drawing back my arm, I received a great wound therein, which I interpreted as a reward for my short-shooting; but, in revenge, I pressed it to him, though I then missed him also, and then received a wound in my right pap both through my body and almost to my back; and then we wrestled for the two greatest and dearest prizes we could expect trial for, honour and life. In which struggling, my hand, having but an ordinary glove upon it, lost one of her servants, though the meanest, which, having hung by a skin, and to sight, yet remaineth as before. At last, breathless, yet keeping our holds, there passed on both sides propositions of quitting each other's swords. But when amity was dead, confidence could not live; and who should quit first was the question, which on neither part either would perform; and wrestling again afresh,

RESPECTFUL ATTENTION

with a kick and wrench together, I freed my long-captivated weapon, which, instantly levelling at his throat – being master still of his — I demanded if he would ask for his life, or yield his sword — both which, though in that imminent danger, he bravely refused to do. Myself being wounded, and feeling loss of blood — having three conduits running on me, which began to make me faint — and he dangerously persisting not to accord to either of my propositions — through remembering his former bloody desire, and feeling my present state, I struck at his heart, but, by his avoiding, missed my aim, yet passed through the body; and, drawing out my sword, repassed it again through another place, when he cried, 'Oh, I am slain!' seconding his speech with all the force he had to cast me. But he being too weak, after I had defended his assault, I easily became master of him, laying him on his back, when, being upon him, I re-demanded if he would request his life, but it seemed he prized it not at so dear a rate to be beholden for it, bravely replying, 'He scorned it,' which answer of his was so noble and worthy, as I protest I could not find it in my heart to offer him any more violence, only keeping him down, until at length his surgeon afar off cried out, 'He would immediately die if his wounds were not stopped.' Whereupon I asked if he desired his surgeon should come, which he accepted of, and so being drawn away, I never offered to take his sword, counting it inhuman to rob a dead man, for so I held him to be. The matter being thus ended, I retired to my surgeon, in whose arms, after I had remained a while, for want of blood I lost my sight, and withal, as I then thought, lost my life also; but strong waters and his diligence quickly recovered me, when I escaped from a very great danger. Lord Bruce's surgeon, when nobody deemed it, came full at me with his lordship's sword, and had not mine, with my sword, interposed, I would have been slain by those base hands.

THE SCANDALMONGER

In spite of the activity of their surgeons, both these noblemen survived.

It would be needless to multiply examples of ferocity in the seventeenth-century duello. There was the Shrewsbury affair, at which Lady Shrewsbury was said to have attended in the costume of a page, on the opposite side to her husband. Lord Buckingham ran the latter through the body, one of the seconds was killed, another severely wounded, two more slightly wounded, and so was Buckingham — but Lady Shrewsbury made up for this, by sleeping with her paramour the same evening, in the bloody shirt which he had worn to skewer her master. There was the infamous young bandit, Lord Mohun, who, after assisting at the murder of an inoffensive actor, fought the Duke of Hamilton in 1712. These two hacked each other to pieces. 'The dog Mohun', wrote Swift, 'was killed on the spot, but while the Duke was over him, Mohun, shortening his sword, stabbed him in at the shoulder to the heart. The Duke was helped towards the lake-house, by the ring, in Hyde Park, where they fought, and died on the grass before he could reach his house, and was brought home in a coach by eight, while the poor Duchess was asleep.' He had received severe wounds in both legs, in one arm and in the right breast, while he had wounded Mohun as fearfully, in groin, arm and body, before receiving his own mortal wound when in the act of exterminating his opponent.

It may be noted that this combat was fought in the eighteenth century: was fought, in fact, in the Age of Reason, though the Age of Scandal had yet to dawn. Even so late as 1743, there was something like a fracas

RESPECTFUL ATTENTION

in the House of Commons, which was described with his usual fun by Walpole.

Pray, Sir, congratulate me upon the new acquisition of glory to my family! We have long been eminent statesmen; now that we are out of employment we have betaken ourselves to war — and we have made great proficiency in a short season... But not to detain you any longer with flourishes, which will probably be inserted in my uncle Horace's patent when he is made a field-marshal; you must know that he has fought a duel, and has scratched a scratch three inches long on the side of his enemy — *Io Paean*! The circumstances of this memorable engagement were, in short, that on some witness being to be examined the other day in the House upon remittances to the army, my uncle said, 'He hoped they would *indemnify* him, if he told anything that affected himself.' Soon after he was standing behind the Speaker's chair, and Will. Chetwynd, an intimate of Bolingbroke, came up to him, and said, 'What, Mr. Walpole, are you for rubbing up old sores?' He replied, 'I think I said very little, considering that you and your friends would last year have hanged up me and my brother at the lobby door without a trial.' Chetwynd answered, 'I would still have you both have your deserts.' The other said, 'If you and I had, probably I should be here and you would be somewhere else.' This drew more words, and Chetwynd took him by the arm and led him out. In the lobby, Horace said, 'We shall be observed, we had better put it off till tomorrow.' 'No, no, now! now!' When they came to the bottom of the stairs, Horace said, 'I am out of breath, let us draw here.' They drew; Chetwynd hit him on the breast, but was not near enough to pierce his coat. Horace made a pass, which the other put by with his hand, but it glanced along his side — a clerk, who had observed them go out together so arm-in-armly, could not believe it amicable, but followed them, and came up just time enough to beat down their swords, as Horace had driven him against a post, and would probably have run him through at the next thrust. Chetwynd went away to a surgeon's, and kept his bed the next day; he has not reappeared yet, but is in no danger. My uncle returned to the House, and was so little moved as to speak immediately upon the *Cambrick Bill*, which made Swinny say, 'That it was a sign he was not *ruffled*.'

These bloodthirsty brawls and improper haggles without seconds had changed to a different tempo in the second half of the century. When Lord Cobham spat in Lord Hervey's hat, as Walpole told in another letter, instead of rushing together as Bazanez and Vallon had done over the same article of dress, Hervey inquired politely, 'Has yr. Lordship any further occasion for my hat?' before setting in hand the proper machinery of challenge. When podgy Charles Fox was to fight with Adam, using pistols, his second, hoping to present a narrower target, said, 'Fox, you must stand sideways.' 'Why, man, I am as thick one way as the other.' Adam desired Fox to fire first; but the latter refused. 'I'll be damned if I do. I have no quarrel.' Adam took the first shot, and wounded his adversary without being aware of the fact. Fox did not fire, refused to apologize in the matter over which they were fighting, and desired his opponent to have another pistol. Adam did so, but missed. Fox fired in the air, and 'mentioned' that he 'believed himself to be wounded'. Charmed with this meiosis, the parties separated. By a curious coincidence, the same pair of pistols was used in a duel between Mr. Fullarton and Lord Shelburne. On being shot in the groin, Lord Shelburne was asked how he did, and replied

RESPECTFUL ATTENTION

gracefully, after inspecting the wound, 'I think that Lady Shelburne will be none the worse for it.' A celebrated duellist, St. Foix, became the hero of as polite an anecdote, related by Franklin. 'A gentleman in a coffee-house desired another to sit further from him. — "Why so?" — "Because, Sir, you smell." — "That, Sir, is an affront, and you must fight me." — "I will fight you if you insist upon it; but I do not see how it will mend the matter; for if you kill me, I shall smell too; and if I kill you, you will smell, if possible, even more than you do at present." '

Ensign Sterne, the gallant father of the author of *Tristram Shandy*, fought a duel with swords, in a room, with a Captain Philips, 'about a goose'. The impetuous captain ran the ensign through the body with so much élan as actually to pin the latter to the wall. Upon this the ensign 'with infinite presence of mind' politely begged the captain to wipe off any pieces of plaster which might adhere to the other end of the sword 'before removing his instrument', since it would be 'disagreeable to have them introduced into his system'.

The tone of battle had changed. People no longer bit each other's chins and rolled about the sward. They were classical in their insult. Not to mince the matter, they were behaving like gentlemen — not like 'Nature's Gentlemen', but like gentlemen: the technical kind which had been defined as dispassionately as one might define a kipper, in medieval books of heraldry. It was the age of literate, articulate aristocrats, who could claim coat armour. 'George III', said Wraxall, 'adopted as a fixed principle that no individual engaged in trade, however ample might be

THE SCANDALMONGER

his nominal fortune, should be created a British peer.'

An example of the new civilization, for comparison with the Duke of Dorset's rough-and-tumble with Lord Bruce, can be found in a letter from Wilkes, describing his own duel with the tetchy Lord Talbot in 1762. Talbot had been a companion of prize-fighters, and was a bully. Gray called him a 'great butcherly lord'. At George III's coronation, it had been his duty as Lord Steward to ride a horse into Westminster Hall — and the horse had to be backed from the presence of the sovereign. Unfortunately, the animal had been taught so well that it also backed into the presence, presenting a fat behind to its monarch, on which the wicked Wilkes had allowed himself to be pleasant in the *North Briton*.

I found his lordship in an agony of passion. He said that I had injured him, that he was not used to be injured or insulted. What did I mean? Did I, or did I not write the *North Briton* of August 21st, which affronted his honour? He would know; he insisted on a direct answer; here were his pistols. I replied that he would soon use them; that I desired to know by what right his lordship catechised me about a paper which did not bear my name. . . .
His lordship then asked me if I would fight him that evening. I said that I preferred the next morning, as it had been settled before, and gave my reasons. His lordship replied that he insisted on finishing the affair immediately. I told him that I should very soon be ready; that I did not mean to quit him, but would absolutely first settle some important business relative to the education of an only daughter, whom I tenderly loved. . . .
I rang the bell for pen, ink and paper, desiring his lordship to conceal his pistols, that they might not be

BLOODY NEWS

RESPECTFUL ATTENTION

seen by the waiter. He soon after became half frantic, and made use of a thousand indecent expressions, that I should be *hanged, damned,* etc. etc. I said that I was not to be frightened, nor in the least affected by such violence; that God had given me a firmness and spirit equal to his lordship's or any man's; that cool courage should always mark me, and that it should be seen how well bottomed *he* was.

After the waiter had brought pen, ink and paper, I proposed that the door of the room might be locked, and not opened till our business was decided. His lordship, on this proposition, became quite outrageous; declared that this was mere *butchery*, and that I was a wretch, who sought his life. I reminded him that I came there on a point of honour, to give his lordship satisfaction; that I mentioned the circumstance of locking the door only to prevent all possibility of interruption. . . .

Soon after he grew a little cooler, and in a soothing tone of voice, said, 'I have never, I believe, offended Mr. Wilkes; why has he attacked me? He must be sorry to see me unhappy.' I asked, upon what ground his lordship imputed the paper to me? That Mr. Wilkes would justify any paper to which he had put his name, and would equally assert the privilege of not giving any answer whatever about a paper which he had not; that this was my undoubted right, which I was ready to seal with my blood. He then said that he admired me exceedingly, really loved me — but I was an unaccountable animal — such parts! but would I kill him who had never offended me? etc. etc. etc. We had after this a good deal of conversation about the Bucks Militia, and the way his lordship came to see us on Wycombe Heath, before I was *colonel*. He soon flamed out again, and said to me, 'You are a murderer, you want to kill me, but I am sure I shall kill you, I know I shall, by G—d! If you *will* fight, if you *will* kill me, I hope you will be *hanged*; I know you will.'

THE SCANDALMONGER

I asked if I was first to be *killed* and afterwards *to be hanged*? That I knew his lordship fought me *with the King's pardon in his pocket*, and I fought him with a halter about my neck; that I would fight him for all that, and if he fell, I should not tarry here a moment for the tender mercies of such a ministry, but would directly proceed to the next stage, where my valet waited for me, and from thence I would make the best of my way to France, as men of honour were sure of protection in that country. He then told me that I was an unbeliever, and *wished* to be killed! I could not help smiling at this, and observed that we did not meet at Bagshot to settle articles of faith, but points of honour. . . .

I then wrote a letter to your lordship respecting the education of Miss Wilkes, and gave you my poor thanks for the steady friendship with which you have honoured me. . . .

When I had sealed my letter, I told his lordship I was entirely at his service, and I again desired that we might decide the affair *in the room*, because there would not be a possibility of interruption; but he was quite inexorable. He then asked me how many times we should fire? I said I left it to his choice; but I had brought a flask of powder and a bag of bullets.

Our seconds then charged the pistols, which my adjutant had brought; they were large horse-pistols. It was agreed that we should fire at the word of command, to be given by one of our seconds. They tossed up, and it fell to my adjutant to give the word. We then left the inn, and walked to a garden at some distance from the house. It was near seven, and the moon shone bright. We stood about eight yards distant, and agreed not to turn round before we fired, but to continue facing each other. Harris gave the word. Both our fires were in very exact time, but neither took effect. I walked up immediately to his lordship, and told him that I now avowed the paper.

RESPECTFUL ATTENTION

His lordship paid me the highest encomiums on my courage, and said he would declare everywhere that I was the noblest fellow God had ever made. He then desired that we might be good friends, and retire to the inn to drink a bottle of claret together, which we did with great good humour, and much laughter.

The deadly calm of Talbot's squinting persecutor, the suggestion that they should fight at short quarters in the room, the explanation of Wilkes's intended movements after his lordship's death, the enormous horse-pistols and the whole bag of bullets, the upsurge of relief to find himself alive, spared by the 'noblest fellow God had ever made', after his vain attempts to terrify at the start: surely no blustering windbag could ever have been so beautifully demoralized! The only consolation was that he deserved it. Wilkes was a perfect surgeon.

'I could not help smiling at this.' Wit had crept into the duel, along with politeness. Another introduction had been the rigid code of behaviour. Indeed, the rules of fighting had been drawn up in Ireland, with the same minuteness as the rules of golf. There were twenty-seven of them. The opening moves, variations and manœuvres had gained a formal elegance like that of a moderately dangerous ballet. Gentlemen who felt themselves to be somewhat in the wrong might 'delope', or fire in the air, like Fox. When they were not liverish like the unhappy Talbot, they could treat each other, even in the act of slaughter, with scrupulous good manners. 'Upon arriving at the *releager*, or place of meeting,' said an authority, 'the challenger should make a point of saluting his antagonist, — again, also, when taking up his position;

and, if his ball takes effect, a third salute, and an expression of regret should always precede his quitting the ground.' A duel between Lord Macartney and General Stewart was fought in 1786, in this spirit. Macartney was short-sighted, but, on Stewart's expressing anxiety lest he should not be able to see to shoot him, he said that he would do as well as he could. He forgot to cock his pistol, was politely reminded to do so by his opponent, and did cock it, after thanking him. At the first fire his lordship was wounded and the seconds endeavoured to stop the fight. Stewart seemed to wish for a further exchange and asked whether his lordship could not endeavour to fire another pistol? Macartney, who had been propped against a tree while the matter was discussed, said that 'he would try with pleasure'. The seconds disapproved, and the matter terminated without further bloodshed.

In addition to the wit, the formality and the politeness which was characteristic of the new Age, there was another trait peculiar to the period. Many duellists had become eccentric. D'Eon, who was a noted swordsman, was thought to be a hermaphrodite. Two women fought in Paris. Men began to meet in gravel pits, in coaches, in the dark. In 1808, an enterprising couple fought in two balloons. By 1843, a meeting had taken place with billiard balls. The balls had to be thrown at each other's heads by hand, and the combatants tossed a coin for the first shy, which proved fatal. The famous duellist Stackpole, on being shot dead by a person called Cecil, observed as he fell: 'By George, I've missed him!'

As a final peculiarity, it was noticed that the duel

had become humane. Where 8000 gentlemen had lost their lives in France, from 1589 to 1608, it has been computed that during the long reign of George III in England, only 69 individuals were killed. These 69 fell in 172 duels, in which 344 persons were concerned, so that only one-fifth of the combatants died. One-half of the duels were bloodless. In 1778, Barney Coyle and George Ogle exchanged eight shots without hitting each other.

By the early part of the nineteenth century, the chances of survival were still higher. From an average of 200 duels, it was found that the odds against being killed were 14 to 1. Against being hit at all, they were 6 to 1. The days of the Chevalier d'Andrieux were over — that chevalier who, in the seventeenth century, had been told by his opponent as they set to work: 'Chevalier, you will be the tenth man I have killed.' 'And you', the Chevalier had replied as he killed him, 'will be my seventy-second.'

There was one other aspect of the subject which may be worth mentioning. Humans are strange creatures — so certain of their superiority to other creatures and even to their own ancestors that it is sometimes salutary to glance upon the other side of the picture. We fight wars about the imaginary lines called frontiers, believing war to be capable of justice and sacrificing the lives of young people by tens of millions, against their will. We have abolished the duel, which used to kill ten men a year in the third George's reign, and we are proud of this great step in civilization, like a dog with two tails.

The duellists, however, did not fight against their wills. They were a negligible number of people — far more committed suicide, for instance, than fought duels — and it has been argued that they served a peculiar function. That function was, to keep society polite. 'To the existence of the Code of Honour introduced by duelling,' said Thomas Moore the poet, who had fought himself, though without much glory, 'we owed very much the great difference between the moderns and the ancients in the good-breeding and decorum of manners in social life. What personal abuse, for instance, what blackguarding . . . Cicero indulged in towards his adversaries.' His point was that, if Cicero had been liable to be called out, he would have confined himself to parliamentary language. 'I have always found', said *The Young Man of Honour's Vade Mecum*, 'that, in the provinces, districts, and cities where the decision of differences by single combat had most prevailed, — for instance, the province of Connaught, city of Dublin, Galway, and some others, — the gentry were the most polite and friendly . . . Where men dare to be rude and insulting, free from the dread of castigation, or being called to account for their conduct in a spirited way, politeness, good-breeding, — nay, common good manners, — are dispensed with.' 'To this absurd custom', said Dr. Robertson, 'we must ascribe, in some degree, the extraordinary gentleness and complacency of modern manners, and that *respectful attention of one man to another*, which, at present, renders the social intercourses of life far more agreeable and decent than among the most civilized nations of antiquity.'

We need not believe that the 'respectful attention' was due to the existence of the 'absurd custom', nor that gentlemen were polite in the Age of Scandal

RESPECTFUL ATTENTION

because they feared each other's swords. They were polite because of the high degree of education which they had enjoyed. It was because they could quote Cicero, and not because they used the épée, that they ended every letter with a newly turned compliment, saying, instead of our perfunctory 'Yours sincerely':

You may be certain that I have many letters to write on this occasion, nor would volumes suffice to tell you, what must be comprised, like an Iliad in a nutshel,
> that I am,
> > my dearest and ever honoured Doctor,
> > > your own
> > > > ORRERY

Even the boorish Dr. Johnson — who approved of duelling — could trouble to make up a letter to his dizzy Bozzy — whose son was killed in a duel — which ended with the laboured grace:

Think only when you see me, that you see a man who loves you, and is proud and glad that you love him.
> I am, Sir,
> > Your most affectionate
> > > SAM. JOHNSON[1]

Sir [wrote some highwayman politely to Horace Walpole, after having nearly shot him], seeing an Advertisement in the papers of to Day giveing an account of your being Rob'd by two Highway men on wednesday night last in Hyde Parke and during the time a Pistol being fired whether Intended or Accidentally was Doubtfull Oblidges us to take this Method of assureing you that it was the latter and by no means Design'd Either to hurt or frighten you.

---

[1] As early as 1804, however, such elegances were already on the decline, and one is grieved to find Lord Charleville writing to his wife in that year as 'Dearest Owney', while signing himself, even more deplorably, as 'Owney Boo'.

THE SCANDALMONGER

It was against a background such as this that the precursor at Florence of Walpole's friend, Sir Horace Mann, took to his bed for six weeks because the Duke of Newcastle had omitted the 'very' in signing a letter to him as 'your (very) humble servant'.

It was against this background that, in the Townshend-Bellamont meeting of 1773, the letters exchanged by the noble seconds all ended by having

The Honour to be,
  My Lord,
    Your Lordship's most
      Obedient and most humble Servant.

The worst insult which the principals were allowed to offer each other in the latter affair was solemnly read from a piece of paper by Lord Charlemont, who recited the following article:

I am enjoined by Lord Bellamont to state to your Lordship, that he considers *you divested* of every principle that *constitutes a man of honour.*

Strong words indeed — and Lord Bellamont paid for them dearly; for he was shot in the groin, which hurt so much that he had to be carried home in a sedan chair; and ever afterwards, we must hope, he was careful not to indulge in Billingsgate.

CHAPTER TWO

A Struggle of Sentiment

THERE was a type thrown up in the late eighteenth century, perhaps because the faculty of 'bottom' was expected from gentlemen. This type was the superman or megalomaniac, who endeavoured to excel his fellows in everything, but particularly in courage. Mytton was such a person; possibly Nelson himself was; but the best example was Thomas Pitt, second Baron Camelford.

The soul of the superman is probably an unhappy one. He believes himself to be a coward at heart, and so, to conceal this, he is forced to prodigies of useless valour. He believes himself to be inferior to his companions; therefore he must force himself to beat them at everything. He detests his own character, so he must seek to make others love it. He is perhaps deeply sincere, with high romantic ideals, self-critical, intelligent and of a sensitive nature. Hating cruelty for sentimental reasons, he observes that he himself is cruel. What he is, he despises; what he is not, he seeks to be.

Camelford was an example of these paradoxes. By birth a rich lord, he treated his title with contempt and sought to be admired as a man. Born to the purple, he disliked his relations and tried to win esteem by being a good carpenter. Educated in the humanities, he turned from them and sought to be a learned mathematician, chemist or theologian. Gentle and probably even soft-hearted by nature, he mistook these virtues for weaknesses and spent much of his life as a bully. 'Over the fire-place in the drawing-room', wrote James and Horace Smith on visiting his house in Bond Street, 'were ornaments strongly expressive of the pugnacity of the peer. A long thick bludgeon lay horizontally supported by two brass hooks. Above this was placed parallel one of lesser dimensions, until a pyramid of weapons gradually arose, tapering to a horse-whip.' Believing himself to be a coward, and that most other people were not cowards, he had to become the second-best pistol-shot in the kingdom, and one of the most dreaded of its duellists. He was forced to be terrible to those who opposed him, while being generous to a fault with those who accepted his leadership. Humble enough to throw away any advantages in his profession — as a naval officer — which came to him by birth or by influence, his satanic pride led him to fight, tooth and nail, for any advantages which he thought he had truly earned. Capable as an officer, and peremptory with his superiors, his high ambition for deserved success was doomed to achieve nothing. Professing infidelity, he made romantic and touching plans for the disposal of his corpse.

Lord Camelford was born in 1775 at Boconnoc in Cornwall, was educated in Switzerland and at Charterhouse, entered the navy at the age of fourteen on a 44-gun ship, was shipwrecked on an ice-field near the Cape of Good Hope, and, when many of the crew had deserted, remained on board with the few who succeeded in bringing the wreck into Table Bay. By the time he was nineteen, he had spent three years on a survey of the north-west coast of America.

A STRUGGLE OF SENTIMENT

Already impatient of discipline at the hands of his technical superiors, he had twice been discharged from his ship by the age of twenty. He was shipwrecked again in 1795 at Ceylon. At twenty-two, he challenged a late captain of his own to a duel, and tried to cane him in the street. This blew over, and he was promoted lieutenant. Before he was twenty-three, he had shot a brother officer in Antigua, over a quarrel about precedence. He was again promoted to the command of a vessel, the *Charon*, and, in 1798, became involved in a peculiar visit to France, with a faint odour of headstrong espionage and treachery. He was tried for this before the Privy Council. He was set at liberty, but the Admiralty, displeased, removed him from his ship. This infuriated Camelford, who had succeeded to the title five years before, and he instantly resigned his commission.

The embittered young nobleman now devoted himself to the life of London. In 1799 he was fined £500 for knocking a Mr. Humphries downstairs. In 1801 he fought a London mob single-handed, with one of his bludgeons. By 1804, when he was not yet thirty, he had 'achieved an extraordinary notoriety by disorderly conduct', was a noted duellist, and was in despair.

The matter for despair was this. If one were warmhearted, one did not enjoy shooting people or kicking them downstairs. If one wanted to be loved and admired, one did not like to realize that people were beginning to hate and to fear one. If one were ambitious, one saw with misery that one's naval career had been ruined. And, worst of all, if one were the second-best pistol-shot in the kingdom one could get

THE SCANDALMONGER

no possible satisfaction from shooting lesser marksmen. It was like potting sitting birds, like striking old men or women, like being the big bully who hits the little boy, because he is smaller than himself.

Camelford saw with self-loathing that he had failed to be a superman, that he had only become a thug, and that he was being classed with ferocious people like Captain Macnamara, who had lately killed a colonel. 'Hayes', noted Farington in his diary, 'spoke of the danger of such men as Lord Camelford and Captn. Macnamara who killed Coll. Montgomery being in Society. No man's life is safe where such men are. A friend of Hayes who is acquainted with Macnamara said that He had killed 3 or 4 men, — that on board ship, He amuses Himself in having fowls that are to be killed placed before him on Hen Coops & He shoots off their Heads with Pistol balls. — To that person, Macnamara said "I am one of the best natured fellows in the world, & yet I do not know how it is, I am always getting into scrapes." — Such are among the characters which are produced in Society!'

The wretched peer perceived the misdirection and wreckage of his hopes, and perceived, at the same moment, that there was only one way out. He disliked himself: so he must punish himself. He doubted his own sadly whipped courage: so he must press it forward once again, to a last proof. He was thought to be a bully for fighting lesser shots: so he must fight a greater one.

If Camelford was a bully, as he certainly was, at least we may be ready to admit that the person whom he bullied most was himself.

A STRUGGLE OF SENTIMENT

There was only one better shot with the pistol, his good friend Mr. Best. It would be necessary to pick a quarrel with him somehow or other — and it would not be very difficult, since they had both kept a Mrs. Simmonds as a mistress. Camelford would tell Best that Mrs. Simmonds had told *him* that Best had told *her* something nasty about Camelford. Then he would demand an apology from Best, for the non-existent nastiness, and there would be no apology, and he would abuse him, and the duel would ensue. He thought the matter over for six weeks.

The following are contemporary accounts:

March 7 [1804]. Hayes came to tea. He had seen Mr. West this afternoon who told him that Lord Camelford was this morning killed in a duel with a Mr. Best a West Indian. — He was afterwards informed of it by another person. . . .
March 10 Westmacott called. He mentioned that Lord Camelford is little regretted. At Lord Darnley's He heard some gentlemen say 'that it was dangerous to sit in company with such a man'. — Mr. Best was very desirous to have made up the quarrel saying, 'that *any apology* for the words Lord Camelford had spoken He wd. accept'. — Lord Camelford had used gross language to Him. Westmacott thinks Lord Camelford was abt. 5 feet 10 inches high, a well looking man, but with rather a *slang manner*. He lodged in Bond-street, & Mrs. Simmonds who He kept had a House *elsewhere*. . . . She is said to have caused the duel by irritating Lord Camelford against Mr. Best. . . .
[Sir George Beaumont] told me that Mr. Best who killed Lord Camelford, immediately rode down to Dunmow to a Mr. Wade's who married His relation and dined there & Had just quitted the place when the Bow street officials arrived in pursuit of him. He had

been up all night and the morning having been wet his Cloaths were very much so but He sat in them. He is a slim person in figure, and not of a strong constitution. He told Mr. Wade that He had *assured Lord Camelford* upon *His word of Honor* that he never uttered the words charged to Him. When they went to the ground Lord Camelford removed from the place they first stopped at to a second & third, objecting to each, at last He fixed upon one & directed His second to measure the ground.

His Lordships second, Mr. Devereux, proposed 8 *paces*; on which Mr. Best's second sd. that He wd. not agree to it, that He did not come there to see them murder each other, & unless they stood at the usual distance viz: 12 *paces*, He wd. quit the ground, on which 12 paces were measured. It was then agreed that Mr. Devereux shd. give the word *to fire*. He did not say *fire* but said '*Be quick*' which Best not understanding to signify *to fire*, did not *instantly*, but Lord Camelford did, and His Ball passed so near Mr. Best's Head that He *heard it*, on which He instantly fired and His Lordship fell — He said farther, that on their *first presenting their pistols* He directed His *wide of Lord Camelford*, who seeing that He did so, said '*That wont do, meaning we are to be in earnest*' — on which Best took an aim, that was fatal. — Mr. Wade took notice that during dinner time a tear started in the eye of Mr. Best. He declared that His conscience was perfectly clear as He did all He could to avoid the duel, & Had He submitted to have put up with the words used by Lord Camelford He was convinced His Lordship wd. have insulted him in any Coffee House. — Carlyle, the Surgeon, told us He was much acquainted with the late Lord Camelford. He said He was a man of superior abilities but of singular character. That his prevailing feeling was *ambition*. — That he had declared to him (Carlyle) that he had no *animal courage* and laboured by any means to get the

A STRUGGLE OF SENTIMENT

better of a weakness of nerves in this respect, by attending Cock-fightings, — pugilism, — &c. &c. That in Him Courage was a struggle of sentiment against Constitution. — He was industrious to acquire knowledge of many things, He was a good Chemist, — a most excellent geographer, — a good seaman, — could do the business of a Turner, & work in *fineering* as a Cabinet Maker. He was very desirous of being reckoned much upon as *a Man* independent of his title & wished His friends to lay that aside and to address Him *familiarly* — But He desired to be at the head notwithstanding — to have the best Horses, — in points of dress, and in other things to be first.

When in a passion it was a kind of phrenzy it disordered Him in so great a degree. — But otherwise His mind was gentle and easy. His generosity was great & *His Charity very extensive.* One person known to Carlyle had paid on charitable accts. more than £11,000 for Him and that to persons who did not know from whence it came. — In political matters He was democratick. He hated all the Royal family except the Prince of Wales who he thought had good qualities. — He disliked Mr. [William] Pitt, *His cousin,* & the whole family of the Grenvilles, though His relations. There had been a grudge, some ill will subsisting between Him & Mr. Best for a month or 6 weeks before the duel & Captain Barrie, His most intimate friend, apprehensive of it producing mischief had urged Lord Camelford to give Him a promise that He wd. not fight Best, which He sd. upon *His Honor He would not.* — When on His death-Bed He reminded Captn. Barrie of His Having broken His word blaming himself for it. — After it had been settled that He was to fight Mr. Best He did all in His power to find Captn. Barrie who was traced to the Play House but unluckily had gone from thence with a Companion & not to His lodgings.

By some means however He was traced and apprized

that Lord Camelford was to fight Best in the morning but He could not learn where they were. At 6 o'Clock He went to Carlyle's who at that early Hour was up, writing. Barrie told him what was going on and regretted that He could not discover where they were, saying that He was certain if present He could prevent the duel. It appeared that in the night Lord Camelford wrote His Will, appointing His sister, Lady Grenville, His Executrix & leaving to Her disposal £150,000. He also directed that His body should be buried in an Island in the Lake of Vevay in Swisserland between 3 *trees* which He specified, adding '*that there Nature might smile on His Bones after the world had forgotten Him*'.

Captain Barrie reached Him very soon after He was carried into the House where He died. He asked Barrie to tell Him truly His situation. Barrie sd. '*Tom you must die*' which He heard with great fortitude. *His sufferings*, & what good He might have done in the world in the midst of His ill, might operate with providence in His favor. He urged Barrie to alter His manner of living & to quit London. He directed that Barrie's debts amounting to £9000 should be paid, and he settled £200 a year upon Him — Lord Grenville was with Him much of the time till His death & their intercourse was kind — He requested Lord Grenville as a gentleman to provide for His *servants*. Captain Barrie was very well satisfied with Lord Grenville's behaviour.

He told Carlyle that on leaving Lord Camelford's room His Lordship said to Him 'That He was entirely unacquainted with Lord Camelford's Will and intentions. That He possessed such abilities that could He have survived 10 years longer till the heat of Youth shd. have passed away & the mind have settled, *He would have been the first Man of the age.*' He left £1000 to purchase a right to a burying ground upon the Island mentioned. — After having wrote His Will &

LORD CAMELFORD

A STRUGGLE OF SENTIMENT

quitted His Lodgings He walked many times round Soho Square in the night in company with a Mr. Nicholson.

FARINGTON

On Sunday, March the 11th, the body of Lord Camelford was opened, when it appeared that the ball had penetrated the right breast between the fourth and fifth ribs, breaking the latter, and making its way through the right lobe of the lungs, into the sixth dorsal vertebra, where it lodged, having completely divided the spinal marrow. In the chest there were upwards of six quarts of extravasated blood.

Eccentric Mirror

After His Lordship's death Lord Grenville wrote to Captn. Barrie in the name of Lady Grenville (Lord Camelford's Sister & Heir) and His own, stating that the friendship subsisting between Lord Camelford & Captain Barrie was known & that they desired that the injunction against Captn. B's residing in London should not be considered by Him as to be attended to, and that the annuity wd. be paid to Him witht. that condition. — In reply Captn. B acknowledged the liberality of Lord & Lady Grenville but declined accepting the annuity, as He could not think of receiving it unless He felt disposed to comply with the condition enjoined by Lord Camelford.

CAPTAIN D'AETH

Several overtures were made to Lord Camelford to produce a reconciliation, but they were rejected with some obduracy. The fact was, his Lordship had an idea that his antagonist was the best shot in England, and he was fearful lest his reputation should suffer, if he made any concession, however slight, to such a person.

REV. WILLIAM COCKBURNE

THE SCANDALMONGER

Steinmetz, never very dependable and not contemporary, added a few details:

He had been questioned as to the names of the gentlemen who had accompanied him, but he declined giving any reply on the subject; and afterwards declared that 'he was the aggressor; that he forgave the gentleman who had shot him, and that he hoped God would forgive him, too.' . . . Lord Camelford, by his will, peremptorily forbade his relatives and friends from prosecuting his antagonist, declaring that the combat was of his own seeking . . . He continued, — 'I wish my body to be removed, as soon as may be convenient, to a country far distant — to a spot not near the haunts of men, but where the surrounding scenery may smile upon my remains.' The place he chose was situated on the borders of the Lake of St. Lampierre, in the Canton of Berne, Switzerland; and three trees stood on the particular spot, as he indicated. The centre tree he desired might be taken up, and, his body being deposited, immediately replaced. *'Let no monument or stone be placed over my grave.'* At the foot of this tree, his lordship added, he formerly passed many solitary hours, contemplating the mutability of human affairs.

In accordance with his desire to be buried in Switzerland, Camelford's body was embalmed and packed in a long basket, but the war prevented its transmission. For many years the body remained in St. Anne's Church, Soho, and eventually disappeared. Camelford never married, and by his death the title became extinct.

JAMES GREIG

CHAPTER THREE

Various Comforters

ONE of the odder foibles of these people was their tender passion for dogs. Pennant listed sixteen kinds:

- I. The most generous kinds
  - Dogs of Chace
    - Hounds: Terrier, Harrier, Blood hound
    - Gaze hound, Grey hound, Leviner, or Lyemmer, Tumbler
  - Fowlers: Spaniel, Setter, Water Spaniel, or finder
  - Lap Dogs: Spaniel gentle, or comforter
- II. Farm Dogs: Shepherd's dog, Mastiff, or ban dog
- III. Mongrels: Wappe, Turnspit, Dancer

Linnaeus explained carefully, if we use Pennant's translation, that:

The dog eats flesh, and farinaceous vegetables, but not greens: its stomach digests bones: it uses the tops of

THE SCANDALMONGER

grass as a vomit. It voids its excrement on a stone: the *album graecum* is one of the greatest encouragers of putrefaction. It laps up its drink with its tongue: it voids its urine sideways, by lifting up one of its hind legs: and is most diuretic in the company of a strange dog. *Odorat anum alterius*: its scent is most exquisite, when its nose is moist: it treads lightly on its toes: scarcely ever sweats; but when hot lolls out its tongue. It generally walks frequently round the place it intends to lye down on: its sense of hearing is very quick when asleep: it dreams. *Procis rixantibus crudelis: catulit cum variis: mordet illa illos: cohaeret copula junctus*: it goes with young sixty-three days; and commonly brings from four to eight at a time; the male puppies resemble the dog, the female the bitch. It is the most faithful of all animals: is very docile: hates strange dogs: will snap at a stone thrown at it: will howl at certain musical notes: all (except the *South American* kind) will bark at strangers: dogs are rejected by the *Mahometans*.

In spite of this erudition, it is difficult to identify the typical lap-dog of the eighteenth century. It was a pug-like, prick- or crop-eared creature, with pop eyes like a pekinese, whose likeness survives in Sir Joshua Reynolds' portrait of Selwyn and Râton, in the possession of the Earl of Rosebery. (The well-known self-portrait of Hogarth, which he altered to satirize Wilkes, contains another example of the same animal.) It would be nice to think that Râton was a Spaniel Gentle — because of the charming pseudonym of 'comforter' — but in that case he may have been barbered for his picture and his ears may have been cut. People always have interfered with the appearance of dogs, without reason, so this is possible.

Whatever the kind, the society of Horace Walpole's

VARIOUS COMFORTERS

period doted on its satellites in a way which had not been seen before in England, even at the court of Charles II. Mrs. Thrale, who was not particularly doggy, had about sixteen of them in the house. Brummell's Duchess of York had upwards of a hundred at Oatlands — not fox-hounds — and a charming St. Bernard once persuaded a friend to write a long petition for him, so that he might be admitted to this sanctuary. Brummell told his landlady: 'Madame de St. Ursain, were I to see a man and a dog drowning together in the same pond, and no one was looking on, I would prefer saving the dog.' Even the Marquis de Sade had a hound which conformed loyally to its master's theories: it ate eight sheep and was called Dragon. Charles James Fox found time to write an epitaph for the Duchess of Devonshire's Faddle. The future Duke of Wellington was, as a young man, 'rather of a weak constitution, not very attentive to his studies, lay about a good deal on a sofa, and was constantly occupied with a little terrier called "Vic" '. The gallant Rodney, shortly before his glorious victory over De Grasse in 1782, took care to send a kiss by post of his 'faithful friend, Loup'. The dogs themselves responded with polite messages, as the Earl of Orrery's Hector did, when he sent Thomas Southerne 'a thousand gentle Wags of his Tail'. Anna Seward called a bitch of hers 'Sweet Sappho', and her butler expired with the final exclamation, 'O! poor Sappho! I can do no more for thee!'

' "A million kisses", wrote Napoleon to Josephine, "even for your horrid Fortune." On their wedding night, the dog was in bed with them. "I had to choose between sleeping beside the beast or not sleeping with my wife. A terrible dilemma, but I had to take it or leave it. I resigned myself. The dog was less accomodating. I have the marks on my leg to shew what he thought about the matter." '

When their masters died, the hounds behaved in the appropriate manner, as was the case with General St. Leger. 'General St. Leger', wrote Hickey, 'brought with him from Europe a large curly-haired, beautifully white dog, of the French breed, that was amazingly attached to him, and a prodigious favourite. This animal had been his inseparable companion for upwards of three years, and had attended him through the whole of the Duke of York's arduous and unfortunate campaign upon the Continent, always sleeping at his feet. When Captain Bradshaw entered the General's room for the purpose of inquiring how he was, he found the dog with his forefoot upon the side of the bed, and licking his master's hand, nor could he by gentle means or any coaxing induce him to leave that position, and when forcibly pulled away he moaned and howled in the most piteous manner. Having been violently dragged from the General's bed and room, he laid himself down at the door, where he remained perfectly quiet until the corpse was carrying out of the house when he set up a low yell, so plaintive and so truly mournful as to draw tears from every soul that heard it . . . On the third morning after the General's death this faithful dog was found dead.'

Sometimes the masters nearly fought duels about them. 'After a sad debauch,' said Hickey in another place, 'about three o'clock in the morning, my party being then reduced to half a dozen, a variety of cold

VARIOUS COMFORTERS

meats, grills, etc., which we had been eating of remaining upon the table, two favourite dogs of mine came to me when, as was my custom, I began to feed them with cold roast beef, which raised the ire of Mr. Burt, who abused me exceedingly . . . Beastly drunk as he certainly was, and, indeed, I was myself far gone, I could not but be surprised at so strange and unexpected an attack upon me. But as I made great allowances to the state he was in and never was quarrelsome myself when in my cups, I was easily persuaded . . . not to take any serious notice of what Mr. Burt had said . . . The day after . . . Mr. Burt was announced . . . Never did I behold a man more truly hurt and distressed than he appeared to be. It seems he had no recollection whatsoever of the circumstance . . . Mr. Burt and I shook hands, he expressing his grateful sense of my good-nature in so readily forgiving his improper behaviour.' At a later date a fatal duel actually did take place, about a dog-fight in Hyde Park. Even the scandalous Duke of Queensberry, the rake of a century, or perhaps of two centuries, except for Richelieu, wrote about his 'canine friends'. (The Duc de Richelieu lived to be ninety-two, and married for the third time in 1780, when he was eighty-four. His only complaint was that the child of this marriage miscarried, and his latest wife had nothing to raise against him, except for his repeated infidelities with other women.) Queensberry, though he scarcely reached the same category, wrote to Selwyn in 1765:

My dear George: I have this moment received your letter from Newark. I wrote to you last night, but I quite forgot Râton. I have not been to see him today, having been the whole morning in the city with

Lady H., but I have sent to your maid, and she says that her *little king* is perfectly well, and in great spirits.

The biographies of favoured pugs can be traced through the correspondence of the period, so that we are able to re-create their lives and deaths, and to perceive the staggering care with which they were treated. If the house had been redecorated, they were boarded elsewhere, lest they should be sickened by the smell of paint: housekeepers were appointed to look after them alone: kisses were busily conveyed to them through the post office by many besides Rodney, indeed by most: in the middle of a war with France, messengers were sent to that country to convey them to England because their French mistresses had died; and great painters were set to work, to make their portraits. As usual, they came to violent ends, because their faith had been seduced. Their lovers had taught them to believe in love, so that they trusted humanity, and the remaining humans proceeded to run them over with their coaches. The heartache of pets had come into being.

At the same time, small boys tortured them, to the fury of Hogarth: wolves ate them when crossing the Alps on the grand tour: the gentle Parson Woodforde calmly hanged them: and occasionally the proletariat took it into its head to get a scare about hydrophobia, and slaughtered as many as it could lay hands on, to the more than fury, to the agony of Horace Walpole.

The commoner sort were called Hector, Caesar, Pompey, etc.: those of the *ton* received French names like Patapan or Tendresse.

Selwyn's pugs were pathetic owing to his love affair with a human baby, Mie-Mie, which cut across the

VARIOUS COMFORTERS

spoiling they had been accustomed to receive. On her appearance, Râton vanished from the correspondence, edited by Jesse, in which he had reigned from 1764 to 1773. 'Madame la Comtesse I hope is well, and *le pauvre Râton,*' his friends had written. 'You may eat boiled chicken and kiss Râton as well on this side of the water as on the other.' 'I thank you, my dear George, for your letter, which I received this morning. It was accompanied by one from Cadogan, who tells me you dined with him, and was covered with Râton's hairs. I hope the Countess owns you have done justice to him, for, in fact, you have thought of nothing but that little son of a —— since you saw her last.' 'I do not believe you would quit Râton's bells for any other avocation whatever.' 'PS. I have a man sits up with me: he shall sit up with your dog all night, and I will watch him all day, rather than that should hinder your coming to Lyons.' 'Râton, likewise, you are silent about. There is in favour at present one of the little naked shivering Italian dogs — the prettiest I ever saw, and has a thousand tricks; I am sure you will love it.' 'I meant to have written you a letter of ceremony only, merely to inquire . . . how the bathing agreed with Râton?' 'It is amazing how little respect he has for dogs. As for me, I assure you I toad-eat a little cur that is here, only because his name is Râton.' 'As you are in a hurry for an answer, and I am thirteen miles distant from Râton, I could not make inquiries about his health to send you; but I will enclose this letter to Richard King, and recommend it to him to inform himself, and slip a note in to give you the intelligence you desire of the *piccolo viso nero.*' 'I had the honour of making Râton a visit, who received me with great acclamations of joy. He looks in perfect health and spirits, and the old woman assures me he is better than ever he was in his life. She made me promise I would write by the last post, to tell you how he did.' 'I rise at six; am on horseback till breakfast; play at cricket till dinner; and dance in the evening till I can scarce crawl to bed at eleven. There is a life for you. You get up at nine; play with Râton till twelve in your night-gown; then creep down to White's to abuse Fanshawe; are five hours at table; sleep till you can escape your supper reckoning; then make two wretches carry you [in a sedan chair] with three pints of claret in you, three miles for a shilling.' 'Your old maid-servant desired I would, with her humble duty, let you know that the little dog is very well, and that she continues to sleep with it at my Lord Carlisle's, lest the smell of the paint should hurt it.' 'Kiss Râton for me.'

So it goes on, through dozens of other letters, until the hunt is up for Mie-Mie; and then even poor Râton's death is not recorded.

Horace Walpole was more faithful to the species. Rosette and Tonton were his, after the death of Patapan. The former of these, Rosette, was a contemporary of Râton's, and it so happened that a play called *Râton et Rosette*, having nothing to do with the dogs, was produced at the Comédie Italienne in Paris. Horace wrote to Selwyn immediately.

Strawberry Hill, Sept. 9, 1771
Who would ever have thought that Râton and Rosette would be talked of for one another? But neither innocence nor age are secure! People say that there never is a smoke without some fire: but here is a striking

proof to the contrary. Only think of the poor dear souls having a comic opera made upon their loves! Rosette is so shocked that she insists upon Râton's posting to Paris, and breaking the poet's bones; *sauf à les ronger après*. If he is a *preux chevalier*, he will vindicate her character *d'une manière éclatante*.

You know I always have some favourite, some successor to Patapan. The present is a tanned black spaniel, called Rosette. She saved my life last Saturday night, so I am sure you will love her too. I was undressing for bed. She barked and was so restless there was no quieting her. I fancied there was somebody under the bed, but there was not. As she looked at the chimney, which roared much, I thought it was the wind, yet wondered, as she had heard it so often. At last, not being able to quiet her, I looked to see what she barked at, and perceived sparks of fire falling from the chimney, and on searching further perceived it in flames. It had not gone far, and we easily extinguished it.

When you write to Spa, pray thank Lord Carlisle for the great civilities I received here. The housekeeper shewed me and told me everything, and even was so kind as to fetch Rosette a basin of water, which completed the conquest of my heart.

My poor Rosette is dying. She relapsed into her fits the last night of my stay at Nuneham, and has suffered exquisitely ever since. You may believe I have too; I have been out of bed twenty times every night, have had no sleep, and sat up with her till three in the morning; but I am only making you laugh at me; I cannot help it — I think of nothing else.

Rosette has suffered dreadfully ever since she was seized at Nuneham; it seems a mixture of complaints, paralytic, and in her bowels. I dare scarce flatter myself with a glimpse of hope! but it is a bad return to give you concern.

THE SCANDALMONGER

You dont flatter me, Madam, by being more concerned for me than for Rosette. She is still alive, but I despair of her recovery. However, you have so little dogmanity that I will say no more about her.

My poor Rosette is better, though I still fear not likely to recover.

The rest of my time has been employed in nursing Rosette — alas! to no purpose. After suffering dreadfully for a fortnight from the time she was seized at Nuneham, she has only languished till about ten days ago. As I have nothing to fill my letter, I will send you her epitaph; it has no merit, for it is an imitation, but in coming from the heart, if ever epitaph did, and therefore your dogmanity will not dislike it.

> Sweetest roses of the year,
> Strew around my Rose's bier.
> Calmly may the dust repose
> Of my pretty faithful Rose!
>
> And if yon cloud-topp'd hill behind,
> This frame dissolved, this breath resign'd,
> Some happier isle, some humbler heaven
> Be to my trembling wishes given,
> Admitted to that equal sky,
> May sweet Rose bear me company!

The most famous of literary dogs, not excepting Mrs. Browning's, was probably Tonton. He belonged to two great people, Madame du Deffand and Horace Walpole, of different nations.

Tonton ... grows the greater favourite the more people he devours. As I am the only person who dare correct him, I have already insisted on his being confined in the Bastille every day after five o'clock. T'other night he flew at Lady Barrymore's face, and I thought would have bitten her eye out; but it ended in biting her finger. She was terrified; she fell into tears. Madame du Deffand, who has too much parts not to see everything in its true light, perceiving that she had not beaten Tonton half enough, immediately told us a story of a lady, whose dog, having bitten a piece out of a gentleman's leg, the tender dame, in a great fright, cried out, 'Won't it make my dog sick?'

My dear old friend [Madame du Deffand] . . . had, indeed, intended to leave me her little all, but I declared I would never set foot in Paris again (this was ten years ago) if she did not engage to retract that destination. To satisfy her, I at last agreed to accept her papers, and one thin gold box with the portrait of her dog. I have written to beg her dog itself, which is so cross, that I am sure nobody else would treat it well.

My poor dear Madame du Deffand's little dog is arrived. She made me promise to take care of it the last time I saw her: that I will most religiously, and make it as happy as is possible.

I told you in my last that Tonton was arrived. I brought him this morning to take possession of his new villa, but his inauguration has not been at all pacific. As he has already found out that he may be as despotic as at Saint Joseph's, he began with exiling my beautiful little cat; upon which, however, we shall not quite agree. He then flew at one of my dogs, who returned it by biting his foot till it bled, but was severely beaten for it. I immediately rung for Margaret [his housekeeper] to dress his foot; but in the midst of my tribulation could not keep my countenance; for she cried, 'Poor little thing, he does not understand my language!' I hope she will not recollect, too, that he is a Papist!

You will find that I have gotten a new Idol — in a word, a successor to Rosette, and almost as great a favourite . . . I dined at Richmond House t'other day, and mentioning whither I was going, the Duke said,

THE SCANDALMONGER

'Own the truth, shall not you call at home first, and see Tonton?' He guessed rightly. He is now sitting on my paper as I write — not the Duke, but Tonton. Do not be afraid, you shall not be plagued with Tonton, though I assure you he has a very decent privy purse for his travels; but I recollect that my uncle Horace used to say that Mademoiselle Furniture does not love dogs; which makes me allow Tonton handsomely, that he may silence such tattling housekeepers as Margaret.

'The Library' I have read. There are some pretty lines and easy verses; but it is too long. One thought is charming, *that a dog, though a flatterer, is still a friend.* It made me give Tonton a warm kiss, and swear it was true.

Good night! I have ordered my bed to be heated as hot as an oven, and Tonton and I must go into it.

Tonton... is not mad, as your Ladyship apprehended, when he bit Lord Ossory's finger; indeed, he can bite but little more than your obedient servant, his master.

I would not interrupt my news, or rather, my replies, and therefore delayed telling you that Tonton is dead, and that I comfort myself: he was grown stone deaf, and very nearly equally blind, and so weak that, the two last days, he could not walk upstairs. Happily, he had not suffered, and died close by my side without a pang or a groan. I have had the satisfaction, for my dear old friend's sake and his own, of having nursed him up, by constant attention, to the age of sixteen, yet always afraid of his surviving me, as it was scarcely possible he could meet a third person who would study his happiness equally. I sent him to Strawberry, and went thither on Sunday to see him buried behind the chapel, near Rosette. I shall miss him greatly, and must not have another dog; I am too old, and should only breed it up to be unhappy, when I am gone. My resource is two marble kittens that Mrs. Damer has given me, of her own work, and which are so much alive that I talk to them, as I did to poor Tonton! if this is being superannuated [he was then seventy-two], no matter: when dotage can amuse itself, it ceases to be an evil.

Another dog was the Earl of Carlisle's Rover, who came to a bad end; though he, like Patapan, had been taken on the Grand Tour, and had met royalty. The fact was that he was travelling with a harum-scarum, though charming, young man, and he appears to have been a little harum-scarum himself.

PS. — Rover is very well, and diverts himself extremely here, but I had near lost him on coming out of Paris; I was obliged to send a servant back three posts for him. When we go post he runs thirty miles, and is then taken into the chaise. Excuse all mistakes, for this is wrote in a great hurry.

I have, according to your desire, given you a detail, and I am afraid a tedious one, of our journey. Rover is very well, and frequently frightened me by standing upon the brink of a precipice to look at the torrent below, the roaring of which he did not in the least comprehend.

Rover is very well, and is perfectly acquainted with Turin: his picture shall be drawn by Pompeio Batroni. I should be very glad to change shapes with Râton for a few hours, when you have a certain company to dinner in Chesterfield Street, but I believe I should behave better than he commonly does.

I take a great deal of exercise, live very regularly, and am very well. Rover is now sitting in the balcony, barking like a cur at all the coaches. He always goes with me to the promenade with a great brick-bat in his mouth.

Rover is extremely well, a great favourite and very amusing to me in my solitude, for I cannot go out without unpacking all my clothes, and that is too much trouble.

I have been in great grief and distress, but am now very easy, about poor Rover: he broke the small bone of his leg by the chaise running, or rather his running under the hind wheel to avoid a great dog that wanted to bite him. It was set immediately, and I have left the only Italian servant I have to nurse him, who is to bring him as soon as the surgeon says he may travel. He was pretty well before I left him.

The Queen of Naples has delayed Rover at Florence, but I hear he is much better, and expect him every day.

I go to Herculaneum tomorrow. If I can possibly steal anything for you I will . . . Rover is come, and pretty well; I hope he will not be lame.

My Dear George: I must begin with desiring you to condole with me upon the unfortunate end of poor Rover, who was run over by a coach and expired immediately. He was buried in the garden; *ibat et ad Stygias nobilis umbra plagas.* Indeed, I am very sorry for him: I never had a dog die a natural death. I will never have another.

'I will never have another.' It was the eternal cry of the bereaved Master. Just as Horace Walpole, as an old man, decided to keep marble animals for the future, so the Earl of Carlisle retreated from the pain of love. Lucretius had summed it up in his lines about Centaurs, pointing out that the animal and the man lived to different ages, and consequently that their union must be impossible.

VARIOUS COMFORTERS

Sed neque Centauri fuerunt, neque tempore in ullo
Esse queat duplici natura, et corpore bino
Ex alienigenis membris compacta potestas . . .
Quae neque florescunt pariter, neque robora sumunt
Corporibus, necque projiciunt aetate senecta.

When Beau Brummell's Vick was dying, with her two doctors, he could not bear to be in the room when she was blooded.

Poor Vick was buried, by his special desire, in Dessin's garden; and though her master did not actually put on mourning, he talked seriously of erecting a monument to her memory. His *salon* was peremptorily closed against visitors for three days, and it was several weeks before he permitted anyone to speak of her death . . . Like a true cynic, his eye was seldom if ever moistened on hearing of the death of a friend, though a flood of tears was always ready when his dogs died.

By Victoria's day the fashionable yet tender craze was waning, and the wits were beginning to do without comforters. Sydney Smith, the most charming of the wits, pretended to detest them. 'No,' he said, 'I don't like dogs; I always expect them to go mad. A lady once asked me for a motto for her dog Spot. I proposed "Out, damned Spot!" but strange to say she did not think it sentimental enough.'

CHAPTER FOUR

Old Schwelly

THE Age of Scandal was, among other things, the first age of the Bluestocking.

'A little Wit is valued in a Woman', the gloomy Dean of St. Patrick's had written in the previous culture, 'as we value a few Words spoken plain by a Parrot.' Now, in the newer period, there were dozens of learned females scattered through the length and breadth of Society, only too anxious to refute his illiberal epigram. Hannah More, Mrs. Thrale, Miss Seward, Fanny Burney, Jane Austen and — the Dr. Johnson of them all — Mrs. Montagu — whose own concessive clauses even she can seldom have hoped to understand — were prattling away in half the drawing-rooms of the kingdom, about morals and metaphysics and history and the derivation of languages.

There was another singular trait of the age — the fashion for the maestro and the disciple: one might almost say, for the guru and the chela. There was Dr. Johnson with his Boswell, Mrs. Thrale with her Burney, Edgeworth with his daughter, Day with Seward, Horace Walpole with Mme du Deffand: even the dear old king had his human satellite, Mrs. Delaney.

Fanny Burney united both these peculiarities. She was, next only to Jane Austen, the greatest female novelist of the century: she was so much of a disciple that her whole life can be traced in sections under one

OLD SCHWELLY

guru or another. She began with Daddy Crisp, who formed her, and passed on through Mrs. Thrale, Dr. Johnson, and Sir Joshua Reynolds to M. D'Arblay — with a distinct slice in between, during which the reigning master of her heart was also the monarch of her country.

Fanny, for all her maidenly ways, was an exhibitionist, or at least she was a successful charmer. She made love to everybody, not physically but by a kind of 'showing off', and she was invariably successful. No, not invariably. Once she failed. Dr. Johnson, Mrs. Thrale, the gallant Frenchman and the rest of them — they all fell at her feet and allowed her to fall at theirs. Her only failure was with Mrs. Schwellenberg, and this failure was due to a frog.

The frog brings us to a third strange feature of the Age of Scandal — the almost preposterous nature of the court of George III. How is it possible, one asks oneself, that they could have had such names? There were Haggerdorn and Papendiek, Mrs. Pohl and Miss Planta, Englehardt, Schnell, Ungerland and Mrs. Theilcke. There were the Misses Gomm, Montmollin and Winklemann, with Pascal, Albert and Dr. Majendie. Even the Princess Royal was nursed by a Mrs. Muttlebury, and Betty Snoswell was the maid.

Mrs. Schwellenberg was the most tremendous, the most preposterous and the most terrible of them all. According to Mrs. Papendiek, the Schwellenberg was 'a shrewd, ambitious woman' who had been with the Queen from infancy — a sort of tyrant Nanny. 'She was to be styled Madame, as a distinction from her companion; her apartments were to join those of the Queen, and no one was to be admitted to her Majesty's

THE SCANDALMONGER

presence without first having been introduced to Madame'. She was accustomed to interfere in minor appointments, and she exasperated Mrs. Papendiek by getting a nomination to the Charterhouse for one of her own nominees, after it had been promised to Mrs. Papendiek's young brother. She had six personal servants. She was incredibly fat. They called her 'old Schwelly'.

In the eighteenth century the word 'family' did not mean 'relations'. It meant 'household', and it included all the footmen and the coachmen and the cook. In this sense, Mrs. Schwellenberg was the head of the Queen's Family — she was the Mistress of the Robes, the head housekeeper, as it were, of all the domestic and other staff. Macaulay, shallow and mistaken as ever, wrote that she was 'a hateful old toad-eater, as illiterate as a chambermaid, as proud as a whole German chapter, rude, peevish, unable to bear solitude, unable to conduct herself with common decency in society'. Fanny Burney described the poor woman in an unpublished part of her diary as 'a companion the most irascible, austere, and superciliously contemptuous to every mode of intercourse that was not of servile obsequiousness'. Horry Walpole, who was always a charming kind of pig, suggested that she had better be given the Garter and made a tutor to the young Prince of Wales, while Bishop Hurd could be the wet-nurse.

Yet this extraordinary old girl had interests almost more varied than those of Fanny herself. For instance, according to the *Eccentric Mirror*, there was a lady named Theodora Grahn, who dressed as a man. Calling herself Dr. John de Verdion, she 'gratified her propensity to drinking to such a degree that she was often seen rolling upon the floor . . . Soon after her arrival in this country, de Verdion became acquainted with Madame Schwellenberg, who is supposed to have been informed of her circumstances and her sex, and to have occasionally assisted her with pecuniary aid'.

This brings the Georgian background to the last astonishment of all — to the dear, mad King himself, who was the summit of the whole learned, hero-worshipping, teutonic, eccentric seraglio. George III was constantly going off his head, when he did or said the most inspired things. 'Was there ever', cried he on one occasion, 'such stuff as great part of Shakespeare? — only, one must not say so! But what think you? What? Is his not sad stuff? What? What?' On another occasion, according to Glenbervie, when going to open the House of Commons, 'he said to the persons in the State Coach with him, "I shall surprise the two Houses by the beginning of my Address to them. I mean to say, 'My Lords and *Peacocks*.' " The attendants were confounded. Some of them ventured to say, "Surely your Majesty would not use the expression." "Yes, but I shall; I shall certainly say 'My Lords and Peacocks.' " He did not, however.' On still another occasion, when he was quite insane, the sacrament was denied to him one Christmas day, for fear of excitement.

Suddenly, in an instant, he got under the sofa, saying that as on that day everything had been denied to him, he would there converse with his Saviour, and no one could interrupt them . . . When he was a little calmer, Mr. Papendiek got under to him, having previously given orders to the attendants that the sofa should be lifted straight up from over them. He remained a moment lying with his Majesty, then by pure strength lifted him in his arms and laid him on his couch.

PAPENDIEK

So much for the background, but now to the dreadful story of Fanny Burney's only failure.

She was a strange little genius, a mental flirt and prim deceiver, a snob, an almost flawless mirror, and a mixture of penetration and duplicity which was irresistible. Until the age of eight, it was said, she had refused to read at all. She had merely sat in the background and observed. Then, at a clap, she had begun to write like a grown-up, overnight. At the age of twenty-six — though she was liable to tell fibs about her age, even to herself, even in her supposedly private diary — she had published anonymously a best-seller, which is still a best-seller. Somehow, by one of those slips which were strangely common to the modest Fanny, this book ceased to be anonymous. Covered with confusion, blushing in her retiring way, gasping with exasperation at the *horrid* publicity, Fanny had succeeded in selling her personality to figures no less important than Johnson, Reynolds and Burke.

But her father was merely an authority on music, she herself was much older than she pretended to be, no suitors seemed to be upon the horizon, money was tight, and, to the little *arriviste* that she really was — for it is quite easy to be socially insincere as well as to be a genius — a life at court seemed to be the summit of ambition. When they offered her a footman, £200 a year (now something like £2000 untaxed), her keep, and a coach — call it a Rolls-Royce

OLD SCHWELLY

— in common with Mrs. Schwellenberg, as assistant Mistress of the Robes, Fanny jumped at the chance with becoming reluctance.

The offer was the usual Hanoverian tribute to genius and integrity. The accepting of it was sensible on Fanny's part. She had charmed everybody with her mental postures, everybody from Daddy Crisp to Sir Joshua Reynolds. There can have seemed to be little reason why she should not charm everybody else, from Mrs. Schwellenberg to Queen Charlotte, and from thence to the King. Fanny accepted, and goodness me, how she tried.

Miss Burney's Rubicon was Mrs. Schwellenberg, for she could not reach to the King and Queen except through her. She sat with that dreadful old Nanny for hours and hours, playing card games which bored her to tears and enduring the draughts which can only be found in a royal palace; she listened to the maddening German accent of her superior till she could have screamed; she effaced herself, she tried to make herself useful; she sat in coaches with the window down — for Nanny was a fresh-air fiend — until her eyes were bloodshot; she endured the humiliation of being offered a cast-off dress of the Queen's; she bridled, she submitted, she secretly criticized, she postured, she almost implored. At a distance of nearly two centuries, we may be permitted to guess that Mrs. Schwellenberg knew exactly what she was at.

Meanwhile there was the etiquette of the astonishing court. There was the ritual dressing of the Queen — always, for Fanny, from the second place. There were the manners which were 'carried so far at Court,

THE SCANDALMONGER

that the Page who wakes the King in the morning does not knock at the door of the bedchamber but what they call *scratches*, that is touches a piece of wood which makes a rattling sound' (Farington). There was the dressing for a Birthday or for a Levée, before which the unfortunate attendants had to go to bed, said Mrs. Mary Frampton, with twenty-four large pins, like hatpins, to control their towering hair-dos. There was the humiliation of never being able to penetrate the defences of Nanny. There were the equerries who had to be given tea and the mental strain of listening to their conversation. Sometimes Mrs. Schwellenberg's shattering attempts at idiom were even worse. Colonel Goldsworthy, for instance, was an equerry who generally went to sleep at teatime — a tea taken alternately by Mrs. Schwellenberg and by Fanny Burney — and this was the kind of conversation which took place afterwards:

A few evenings ago, she very gravely said, 'Colonel Goldsworthy always sleeps with me! Sleeps he with you the same?'
... It was with difficulty I could keep my countenance at this question, which I was forced to negative. The next evening she repeated it — 'Vell, sleeps he yet with you — Colonel Goldsworthy?'
'Not yet, ma'am,' I hesitatingly answered.

BURNEY

Fanny defended herself secretly, as best she could, by writing in her wonderful Journal a bitter caricature of Mrs. Schwellenberg — whom she called Cerbera, with unconscious truth. Cerberus was the guardian of a place, and Fanny could not win past her to it.

At last it all became plain. It was no use wooing

OLD SCHWELLY

Mrs. Schwellenberg: it was no use posturing before her in the bluestocking colours of the butterfly which had charmed the hearts of gurus like Dr. Johnson: the best thing was to give in, to leave the Palace, to retire defeated into some literary life. This retreat Fanny made.

But what hurt her most was to realize what the agency was by which she had been defeated. The daughter of Dr. Burney the musician, the author of *Evelina*, the friend of Burke, had been defeated by a series of frogs. The Cerbera was more interested in natural history than in the romantic stories of female novelists. She was a collector of batrachians.

What a stare was drawn from our new equerry by Major Price's gravely asking Mrs. Schwellenberg after the health of her frogs! She answered they were very well, and the Major said, 'You must know, Colonel Gwynn, Mrs. Schwellenberg keeps a pair of frogs.'
'Of frogs! — pray what do they feed upon?'
'Flies, sir!' she answered.
The stare was now still wider.
'But I can make them croak when I will,' she added, 'when I only go so to my snuff-box, knock, knock, knock, they croak all what I please.'
'Very pretty, indeed,' exclaimed Colonel Goldsworthy.
'I thought to have some spawn,' she continued, 'but Lady Mary Carlton, what you call Lady Doncaster, came and frightened them; I was never so angry!'
'I am sorry for that,' said the Major, very seriously, 'for else I should have begged a pair.' . . .
Then followed a formal enumeration of the frog's virtues and endearing little qualities which made all laugh except the new equerry, who sat in perfect amaze.

BURNEY

CHAPTER FIVE

Dry Blood and Distant Thunder

WHEN I glance in a newspaper [wrote Horace Walpole in 1784], on an article of a report on convicts, I hide the paragraph with my finger, that I may not know the day of execution, and feel for what wretches, whom I cannot help, are feeling.

He had reason to avert his eyes from much of the life which surrounded him, as a quotation from the *Dictionary of National Biography* may show:

HODGE, ARTHUR (d. 1811), West Indian planter, settled about 1792 in Tortola, the chief of the Virgin Islands in the West Indies. He occupied the estate of Bellevue, in the eastern part of the island. Though a man of quarrelsome character, he rose to be a member of council for the dependency of the Virgin Islands. In 1803 the negroes on his estate numbered 140, but in 1811 they numbered only thirty-five, and the diminution was attributed to Hodge's cruelties. Early in 1811 a free negro woman named Perreen Georges deposed before three justices of the peace for Tortola that from 1805 to 1807 she had been in occasional employment at Bellevue. During that period, she declared, three negroes named Tom Boiler, Prosper and Cuffy had been flogged at Hodge's orders with such severity that they all died within a few days of their punishment. Two female slaves named Margaret and Else, accused, for no reason it seems, of trying to poison Hodge's children, had been murdered by having boiling water forced down their throats. Lastly, a child named Samson had been flayed alive by being dipped in a cauldron of scalding water. Astonished at this catalogue of horrors, the justices summoned before them one Stephen M'Keough, formerly overseer on Hodge's plantation, then resident in the Danish island of St. Croix. M'Keough not only corroborated Perreen's statements, but brought forward numerous additional charges of gross cruelty. The justices arrested and prosecuted Hodge on a charge of murder. Five distinct counts were stated in the indictment. The case of the negro Prosper was proceeded with first. The trial began on 29 April before a special court of oyer and terminer and gaol delivery, presided over by Mr. Hetherington. Perreen Georges and M'Keough gave evidence showing that Prosper, having been accused of pulling a mango from a tree, and being unable to find the six shillings which Hodge demanded as compensation, had been laid down and cart-whipped for the space of one hour; that he next day had been tied to a tree and flogged 'at short quarters', i.e. with a short-looped lash, till he fainted; that he had then been chained up with two other negroes; and that, while his comrades managed to escape, he himself crawled into a hut, where he died unattended. M'Keough declared that sometimes two or three negroes died in a single night. Among corroborative witnesses was Mrs. Rawbone, Hodge's sister. The defence tried in vain to discredit the witnesses, and appealed to the jury in the name of Hodge's young family. The jury brought in a verdict of guilty, and Hodge was sentenced to death. He spent the last days of his life in religious exercises, and suffered the extreme penalty of the law on 8 May 1811.

Probably the atrocities of this madman may still be remembered in the West Indies as an example of English cruelty to negroes, just as every rebel in Ireland is remembered as an example of English ferocity. It never suits the agitator to remember that

THE SCANDALMONGER

the negroes, the Irish and the English too, were as ferocious to themselves, in the eighteenth century, as they were to one another. For the Age of Scandal, while being on the one hand romantic and sentimental to the verge of tears, was at the same time drenched in blood. 'Here,' wrote Goldsmith:

Here, while the proud their long-drawn pomps display,
There, the black gibbet glooms beside the way.

Wherever the patrician drove in the countryside of England, he could still pass a gallows: looking up, at bridges and gateways, he could meet the empty eye-sockets of beheaded men. As late as 1772, there were heads on Temple Bar. The famous Eugene Aram was hanged in chains at Knaresborough in 1759, and his wife continued to live in the parish; she picked up the bones as they dropped, while his children conducted strangers to view the gibbet. Torture was used in 1721, when a man was 'pressed' because he had refused to plead, and was not abolished until 1772. The axe was still in action, and Walpole's descriptions of the peers who were executed, from the lunatic Ferrers to the rebel lords like Lovat, Kilmarnock and Balmerino, were among the most vivid in his letters.

What will your Italians say to a peer of England, an earl of one of the best families, tried for murdering his servant, with the utmost dignity and solemnity, and then hanged at the common place of execution for highwaymen, and afterwards anatomized? . . . His misfortunes, as he called them, were dated from his marriage, though he had been guilty of horrid excesses unconnected with matrimony, and is even believed to have killed a groom who died a year after receiving a cruel beating from him. His wife, a very pretty woman, sister to Sir William Meredith, had no fortune,

DRY BLOOD AND DISTANT THUNDER

and he says, trepanned him into marriage, having met him drunk at an assembly in the country, and kept him so till the ceremony was over. As he always kept himself so afterwards, one need not impute it to her . . . He had a mistress [Mrs. Clifford] before and two or three children, and her he took again after the separation from his wife. He was fond of both, and used both ill: his wife so ill, always carrying pistols to bed, and threatening to kill her before morning, beating her, and jealous without provocation, that she got separated from him by act of Parliament, which appointed receivers of his estate in order to secure her allowance. This he could not bear. However, he named his steward for one, but afterwards finding out that this Johnson had paid her fifty pounds without his knowledge, and suspecting him of being in a confederacy against him, he determined, when he failed of opportunities of murdering his wife, to kill the steward . . . The shocking circumstances attending the murder, I did not tell you . . . Having shot the steward at three in the afternoon, he persecuted him till one in the morning, threatening again to murder him, attempting to tear off his bandages, and terrifying him till in that misery he was glad to obtain leave to be removed to his own house; and when the Earl heard the poor creature was dead, he said he gloried in having killed him . . . Dr. Munro since the trial has made an affidavit of his lunacy . . . On the last morning he dressed himself in his wedding clothes, and said he thought this, at least, as good an occasion for putting them on as that for which they were first made. He wore them to Tyburn. This marked the strong impression on his mind . . . He set out from the Tower at nine, amidst crowds, thousands. First went a string of constables; then one of the Sheriffs, in his chariot and six, the horses dressed with ribbons; next Lord Ferrers, in his own landau and six, his coachman crying all the way; guards at each side; the other sheriff's chariot followed empty, with a mourning-coach and six, a hearse, and the Horse Guards. Observe, that the empty chariot was that of the other sheriff, who was in the coach with the prisoner, and who was Vaillant, the French bookseller in the Strand. How will you decipher all these strange circumstances to Florentines? A bookseller in robes and in mourning, sitting as a magistrate by the side of the Earl; and in the evening everybody going to Vaillant's shop to hear the particulars. I wrote to him, as he serves me, for the account; but he intends to print it, and I will send it to you with some other things, and the trial. Lord Ferrers at first talked on indifferent matters, and observing the prodigious confluence of people, (the blind was drawn up on his side) he said, — 'But they never saw a lord hanged, and perhaps will never see another.' One of the dragoons was thrown by his horse's leg entangling in the hind wheel: Lord Ferrers expressed much concern, and said, 'I hope there will be no death today but mine,' and was pleased when Vaillant told him the man was not hurt. Vaillant made excuses to him on his office. 'On the contrary,' said the Earl, 'I am much obliged to you. I feared the disagreeableness of the duty might make you depute your under-sheriff. As you are so good as to execute it yourself, I am persuaded the dreadful apparatus will be conducted with more expedition.' The chaplain of the Tower, who sat backwards, then thought it his turn to speak, and began to talk on religion; but Lord Ferrers received it impatiently. However, the chaplain persevered, and said, he wished to bring his Lordship to some confession or acknowledgement of contrition for a crime so repugnant to the laws of God and man, and wished him to endeavour to do whatever could be done in so short a time. The Earl replied, 'He had done everything he proposed to do with regard to God and man; and as to discourses on religion, you and I, Sir,' said he to the

clergyman, 'shall probably not agree on that subject. The passage is very short; you will not have time to convince me, nor I to refute you; it cannot be ended before we arrive.' The clergyman still insisted, and urged, that, at least, the world would expect some satisfaction. Lord Ferrers replied, with some impatience, 'Sir, what have I to do with the world? I am going to pay a forfeit life, which my country has thought proper to take from me — what do I care now what the world thinks of me? But, Sir, since you do desire some confession, I will confess one thing to you: I do believe there is a God. As to modes of worship, we had better not talk on them. I always thought Lord Bolingbroke in the wrong to publish his notions on religion; I will not fall into the same error.' The chaplain, seeing sensibly that it was in vain to make any more attempts, contented himself with representing to him, that it would be expected from one of his calling, and that even decency required, that some prayer should be used on the scaffold, and asked his leave, at least to repeat the Lord's Prayer there. Lord Ferrers replied, 'I always thought it a good prayer; you may use it if you please.'
While these discourses were passing, the procession was stopped by the crowd. The Earl said he was dry, and wished for some wine and water. The sheriff said, he was sorry to be obliged to refuse him. By late regulations they were enjoined not to let prisoners drink from the place of imprisonment to that of execution, as great indecencies had been formerly committed by the lower species of criminals getting drunk; 'And though,' said he, 'my Lord, I might think myself excusable in overlooking this order out of regard of your Lordship's rank, yet there is another reason which, I am sure, will weigh with you: — your Lordship is sensible of the greatness of the crowd: we must draw up to some tavern; the confluence would be so great, that it would delay the expedition which your

THE SCANDALMONGER

Lordship seems so much to desire.' He replied, he was satisfied, adding, — 'Then I must be content with this,' and took some pigtail tobacco out of his pocket. As they went on, a letter was thrown into his coach; it was from his mistress, to tell him, it was impossible, from the crowd, for her to get up to the spot where he had appointed her to meet and take leave of him, but that she was in a hackney-coach of such a number. He begged Vaillant to order his officers to try to get the hackney-coach up to his. 'My Lord,' said Vaillant, 'you have behaved so well hitherto, that I think it is pity to venture unmanning yourself.' He was struck, and was satisfied without seeing her. As they drew nigh, he said, 'I perceive we are almost arrived; it is time to do what little more I have to do;' and then taking out his watch, gave it to Vaillant, desiring him to accept it as a mark of his gratitude for his kind behaviour, adding, 'It is scarce worth your acceptance; but I have nothing else; it is a stop-watch, and a pretty accurate one.' He gave five guineas to the chaplain, and took out as much for the executioner. Then giving Vaillant a pocket book, he begged him to deliver it to Mrs. Clifford his mistress, with what it contained, and with his most tender regards, saying, 'The key of it is to the watch, but I am persuaded you are too much of a gentleman to open it.' He destined the remainder of the money in his purse to the same person, and with the same tender regards.
When they came to Tyburn, his coach was detained some minutes by the conflux of people; but as soon as the door was opened, he stepped out readily and mounted the scaffold; it was hung with black, by the undertaker, and at the expense of his family. Under the gallows was a new-invented stage, to be struck from under him. He showed no kind of fear or discomposure, only just looking at the gallows with a slight motion of dissatisfaction. He said little, kneeled for a moment to the prayer, said, 'Lord have mercy

ILLUSTRATION FROM TYBURN CHRONICLE

upon me, and forgive me my errors,' and immediately mounted the upper stage. He had come pinioned with a black sash, and was unwilling to have his hands tied, or his face covered, but was persuaded to both. When the rope was put round his neck, he turned pale, but recovered his countenance instantly, and was but seven minutes from leaving the coach, to the signal given for striking the stage. As the machine was new, they were not ready at it, and he suffered a little, having had time, by their bungling, to raise his cap; but the executioner pulled it down again, and they pulled his legs, so that he was soon out of pain, and quite dead in four minutes. He desired not to be stripped and exposed, and Vaillant promised him, though his clothes must be taken off, that his shirt should not. This decency ended with him: the sheriffs fell to eating and drinking on the scaffold, and helped up one of their friends to drink with them, as he was still hanging, which he did for above an hour, and then was conveyed back with the said pomp to Surgeon's Hall, to be dissected. The executioners fought for the rope, and the one who lost it cried. The mob tore off the black cloth as relics; but the universal crowd behaved with great decency and admiration, as they well might; for sure no exit was ever made with more sensible resolution and with less ostentation.

The rebel lords were decapitated in 1746 for their part in the last attempt of the Stuarts to regain the English throne.

Just before they came out of the Tower, Lord Balmerino drank a bumper to King James's health. As the clock struck ten, they came forth on foot, Lord Kilmarnock all in black, his hair unpowdered in a bag, supported by Forster, the great Presbyterian, and by Mr. Hume, a young clergyman, his friend. Lord Balmerino followed, alone, in a blue coat, turned up with red (his rebellious regimentals,) a flannel waistcoat, and his shroud beneath; their hearses following. They were conducted to a house near the scaffold: the room forwards had benches for spectators, in the second Lord Kilmarnock was put, and in the third backwards Lord Balmerino: all three chambers hung with black. Here they parted! Balmerino embraced the other, and said, 'My Lord, I wish I could suffer for both!' He had scarce left him, before he desired to see him again, and then asked him, 'My Lord Kilmarnock, do you know anything of the resolution taken in our army, the day before the battle of Culloden, to put the English prisoners to death?' He replied, 'My Lord, I was not present; but since I came hither, I have had all the reason in the world to believe that there was such order taken; and I hear the Duke has the pocket book with the order.' Balmerino answered, 'It was a lie raised to excuse their barbarity to us.' — Take notice, that the Duke's charging this on Lord Kilmarnock (certainly on misinformation), decided this unhappy man's fate! The most now pretended is, that it would have come to Lord Kilmarnock's turn to have given the word for the slaughter, as lieutenant-general, with the patent for which he was immediately drawn into rebellion, after having been staggered by his wife, her mother, his own poverty, and the defeat of Cope. He remained an hour and a half in the house, and shed tears. At last he came to the scaffold, certainly much terrified, but with a resolution that prevented his behaving in the least meanly or unlike a gentleman. He took no notice of the crowd, only to desire that the baize might be lifted up from the rails, that the mob might see the spectacle. He stood and prayed some time with Forster, who wept over him, exhorted and encouraged him. He delivered a long speech to the Sheriff, and with a noble manliness stuck to the recantation he had made at his trial; declaring he wished that all who embarked in the same cause might meet the same fate.

DRY BLOOD AND DISTANT THUNDER

He then took off his bag, coat and waist coat, with great composure, and after some trouble put on a napkin-cap, and then several times tried the block; the executioner, who was in white, with a white apron, out of tenderness concealing the axe behind himself. At last the Earl knelt down, with a visible unwillingness to depart, and after five minutes dropped his handkerchief, the signal, and his head was cut off at once, only hanging by a bit of skin, and was received in a scarlet cloth by four of the undertaker's men kneeling, who wrapped it up and put it into the coffin with the body; orders having been given not to expose the heads, as used to be the custom.

The scaffold was immediately new-strewed with saw-dust, the block new-covered, the executioner new-dressed, and a new axe brought. Then came old Balmerino, treading with the air of a general. As soon as he mounted the scaffold, he read the inscription on his coffin, as he did again afterwards: he then surveyed the spectators, who were in amazing numbers, even upon masts of ships in the river; and pulling out his spectacles read a treasonable speech, which he delivered to the Sheriff, and said, the young Pretender was so sweet a prince, that flesh and blood could not resist following him; and lying down to try the block, he said, 'If I had a thousand lives, I would lay them all down here in the same cause.' He said, if he had not taken the sacrament the day before, he would have knocked down Williamson, the lieutenant of the Tower, for his ill usage of him. He took the axe and felt it, and asked the headsman how many blows he had given Lord Kilmarnock; and gave him three guineas. Two clergymen, who attended him, coming up, he said, 'No, gentlemen, I believe you have already done me all the service you can.' Then he went to the corner of the scaffold, and called very loud for the warder, to give him his perriwig, which he took off, and put on a night-cap of Scotch plaid, and then pulled off his coat and waistcoat and lay down; but being told he was on the wrong side, valuted round, and immediately gave the signal by tossing up his arm, as if he were giving the signal for battle. He received three blows, but the first certainly took away all sensation. He was not a quarter of an hour on the scaffold; Lord Kilmarnock above half a one. Balmerino certainly died with the intrepidity of a hero, but with the insensibility of one too. As he walked from his prison to execution, seeing every window and top of house filled with spectators, he cried out, 'Look, look, how they are all piled up like rotten oranges!'

The fact of the matter was that during the Age of Scandal the British Islands were still to a large extent shackled by Tudor legislation — France, where Damien could be dragged in pieces by horses, was even further behind — and it might not be too much to say that Walpole, in describing death by the axe on Tower Green, or by the silken rope of the frantic Ferrers, was a bridge between modern criminal law and that of Henry VIII. Indeed, a Queen of England was tried by the Lords as late as 1819, for an offence which, had she been found guilty, should have resulted in the same fate as Anne Boleyn's. Colonel Despard's head was cut off, after hanging, for high treason, as recently as 1803, and so was Thistlewood's in 1820. The last English witch legally convicted may have been Jane Wenham in 1712, but in 1751 a poor old couple were ducked to death for witchcraft by a mob near Tring. In 1753 a woman was burned at the stake for petty treason because she had poisoned her husband. We should commiserate her punishment the more if she had not added insult to injury by administering the arsenic in a bowl of gruel — a form of nourishment which her husband detested. The *Newgate Calendar* gave an excellent picture of her incineration, showing the toes curled up to escape the flames, and described her case with gusto.

The behaviour of this fiend had long been a prelude to the diabolical crime which she committed. She was in her family turbulent and dictatorial; her husband the very reverse. His mild and quiet disposition served only to nurse her opposition and violence. He had long given way to her in all things, and she, in return, ruled him with a rod of iron.
Before the commission of this horrid deed we have found women make use of man's unqualified indulgence. Hence arose the vulgar saying of 'the grey mare being the better horse', of 'hen-pecked husbands', and many other irritating observations on men troubled with shrews.
One of the wisest of the ancient philosophers had his Xantippe: and the poet sings,

> When man to woman gives the sway,
> To what is right they oft say Nay.

The pliancy of the more unfortunate man in question could not shield him from the consequence of the ascendancy she had over him; it sunk into contempt, and she determined to rule alone. To effect this, her wicked heart suggested the death of her husband. For this horrid purpose she prevailed on their servant-man to purchase some white mercury, which she mixed in some gruel, and caused him to eat it. This mode of administering the poison, it was conjectured, was adopted in contempt of him; for it appeared the poor man did not like gruel. She then directed him to draw her some ale, of which he also drank; and was immediately seized with violent purgings and vomiting. She told the man, whom it seems she meant afterwards to share her bed, that she 'had given her

THE SCANDALMONGER

husband the stuff he bought, and that it was operating purely'.

The dying man, in his agonies, said his wife was a wicked woman; that he was well until she made him eat some pap, which had done his business, and that he should be a dead man on the morrow; and, in spite of medical aid, he died next day, his body being in a state of mortification.

The horrid crime being fully proved against her, she received sentence to be burnt at the stake, which sentence was accordingly carried into execution at Gloucester, April 13, 1753, among a number of spectators, who showed little pity for her fate, and which became still more shocking from denying the fact, so incontrovertibly proved, to the very last moment of her existence.

Ann Beddingfield was burnt for a similar crime as late as 1763, though in both these cases the women were probably strangled with a rope, the moment the fire had been lighted. Catherine Hayes, however, in 1726,

was literally burnt alive; for the executioner letting go the rope sooner than usual, in consequence of the flames reaching his hands, the fire burnt fiercely round her, and the spectators beheld her pushing away the faggots, while she rent the air with her cries and lamentations. Other faggots were instantly thrown on her; but she survived amidst the flames for a considerable time, and her body was not perfectly reduced to ashes in less than three hours.

The stake was the legal punishment for murdering a husband — petty treason — until 1790.

A few illustrations [says Lecky] will sufficiently show the extravagant absurdity of the [eighteenth-century] criminal code. Thus, to steal a sheep or a horse; to snatch a man's property out of his hands and run away with it; to steal to the amount of forty shillings in a dwelling-house, or to the amount of five shillings 'privately' in a shop; to pick a man's pocket of any greater sum than twelve pence; to steal linen from a bleaching ground, and woolen cloth from a tenter ground; to cut down trees in a garden or in an orchard, to break the border of a fish-pond so that the fish may escape, were all crimes punishable with death. On the other hand, it was not a capital offence for a man to attempt the life of his father; to commit premeditated perjury, even when the result was the execution of an innocent man; to stab a man, however severely, provided the victim did not die from the wound; to burn a house in which the incendiary had a lease, even though it was so situated as to endanger the lives of hundreds. It was a capital offence to steal goods to the amount of forty shillings from a vessel on a navigable river, but not from a vessel on a canal. To steal fruit ready gathered was a felony. To gather it and steal it was only a trespass. To break a pane of glass at five in the afternoon for the purpose of stealing something that lay in the window was a capital offence. To break open a house with every circumstance of violence in summer, at four o'clock in the morning, was only a misdemeanour. To steal goods from a shop, if the thief happened to be seen to take them, was punishable by transportation. To steal the same goods 'privately', that is to say when the criminal was not seen, was punishable by death. In one case a servant was put on his trial who had attempted to murder his master, and had given him fifteen wounds with a hatchet. He was executed, not as an attempted murderer, but as burglar, because he had been obliged to lift up the latch of his master's door in order to enter his chamber. In another case a man of notoriously bad character, after going through a course of burglary and larceny with impunity, was at last convicted and executed for cutting down young trees ... A natural result of such laws was the constant perjury of juries. Unwilling to convict culprits for small offences which were made punishable by death, they frequently acquitted in the face of the clearest evidence.

It appears still to have been the rule [he says later] that criminal trials should be compressed into a single day ... In the more lucrative branches of the profession no such hurry was shown. Civil suits, and especially suits in Chancery, were often protracted for years, and sometimes even for generations, by merciless legal subtleties, and in this way countless fortunes were engulfed, and countless hearts were broken. But in those less lucrative cases in which only a human life was pending, evidence was often hurried through with indecent haste.

A cause of much evil [wrote the author of *Thoughts on Executive Justice*], is the trying prisoners after dinner, when from the morning's adjournment all parties have retired to a hearty meal, which at assize time is commonly attended, among the middling and lower ranks of people at least, with a good deal of drink ... Drunkenness is too frequently apparent where it ought of all things to be avoided. I mean in jurymen and witnesses. The heat of the court, joined to the fumes of the liquor, has laid many an honest juryman into a calm and profound sleep, and sometimes it has been no small trouble for his fellows to jog him into the verdict, even where a wretch's life has depended on the event.

It may seem heartless to make amusement out of the gallows and its human dread; but the fact remains that the eccentricity of Walpole's contemporaries was so pervasive, the oddity of their individual and vigorous attitude so strong, that the ridiculous and the unexpected penetrated even to the macabre. One

DRY BLOOD AND DISTANT THUNDER

hangman cried, as we have seen, because he had lost his perquisites; another stopped half way through the execution to make sure of a handkerchief which the criminal had dropped; a third found it easier to dispense with the gallows altogether. This was

the celebrated Lieutenant Heppenstal, who, in the year 1798, acquired the surname of the *walking gallows* from the following circumstance; he was a remarkably tall, robust man, and had a habit of expertly executing straggling Rebels, when he happened to meet them, by twisting his own cravat round their necks, then throwing it over his own brawny shoulder, and so trotting about at a smart pace, with the Rebel dangling at his back, and choking gradually till he was totally defunct, which generally happened before the Lieutenant was tired of his amusement.

BARRINGTON

Nor did the executioners always have matters their own way. Sometimes, as in the case of Half-hanged Smith, they had trouble with a deceitful audience.

John Smith ... was the son of a farmer at Malton, about fifteen miles from the city of York, who bound him apprentice to a packer in London, with whom he served out his time, and afterwards worked as a journeyman. He then went to sea in a merchant-man, after which he entered on board a man of war, and was at the famous expedition against Vigo; but on the return from that expedition he was discharged.

He had not long been disengaged from the naval service when he enlisted as a soldier in the regiment of Guards commanded by Lord Cutts; but in this station he soon made bad connexions, and engaged with some of his dissolute companions as a housebreaker.

On the 5th of December, 1705, he was arraigned on four different indictments, on two of which he was convicted. While he lay under sentence of death he seemed very little affected with his situation, absolutely depending on a reprieve, through the interest of his friends.

However, an order came for his execution on the 24th day of the same month, in consequence of which he was carried to Tyburn, where he performed his devotions, and was turned off in the usual manner; but when he had hung near fifteen minutes, the people present cried out, 'A reprieve!' Hereupon the malefactor was cut down, and, being conveyed to a house in the neighbourhood, he soon recovered, in consequence of bleeding and other proper applications.

When he perfectly recovered his senses, he was asked what were his feelings at the time of execution; to which he repeatedly replied, in substance, as follows: 'That when he was turned off, he, for some time, was sensible of very great pain, occasioned by the weight of his body, and felt his spirits in a strange commotion, violently pressing upwards; that having forced their way to his head, he, as it were, saw a great blaze, or glaring light, which seemed to go out at his eyes with a flash, and then he lost all sense of pain. That after he was cut down, and began to come to himself, the blood and spirits, forcing themselves into their former channels, put him, by a sort of pricking or shooting, to such intolerable pain that he could have wished those hanged who had cut him down.' From this circumstance he was called 'Half-hanged Smith'.

After this narrow escape from the grave, Smith pleaded to his pardon on the 20th of February; yet such was his propensity to evil deeds, that he returned to his former practices, and, being apprehended, was tried at the Old Bailey, for housebreaking; but some difficulties arising in the case, the jury brought in a special verdict, in consequence of which the affair was left to the opinion of the twelve judges, who determined in favour of the prisoner.

After this second extraordinary escape, he was a

DRY BLOOD AND DISTANT THUNDER

third time indicted; but the prosecutor happening to die before the day of the trial, he once more obtained that liberty, which his conduct showed he had not deserved.

We have no account what became of this man after this third remarkable incident in his favour; but Christian charity inclines us to hope that he made a proper use of the singular dispensation of Providence evinced in his own person.

Newgate Calendar

Sometimes the executioners had trouble with the clients.

We have adduced many instances of the hardness of heart, and contempt of the commandments of God, in men who have undergone the last sentence of the law; but we are of opinion that this *female* will be found a more relentless heart, in her last moments, than any criminal we have yet recorded.

Hannah Dagoe was born in Ireland, and was one of that numerous class of women who ply at Covent Garden Market, to the exclusion of poor Englishwomen.

She became acquainted with a poor and industrious woman of the name of Eleanor Hussey, who lived by herself in a small apartment, in which was some creditable household furniture, the remains of the worldly goods of her deceased husband. Seizing an opportunity, when the owner was from home, this daring woman broke into Hussey's room, and stripped it of every article which it contained.

For this robbery and burglary she was brought to trial at the Old Bailey, found guilty, and sentenced to death. She was a strong masculine woman, the terror of her fellow-prisoners, and actually stabbed one of the men who had given evidence against her; but the wound happened not to prove dangerous.

On the road to Tyburn she showed little concern at

her miserable state, and paid no attention to the exhortations of the Romish priest who attended her. When the cart in which she was bound was drawn under the gallows she got her hands and arms loose, seized the executioner, struggled with him, and gave him so violent a blow on the breast as nearly knocked him down. She dared him to hang her, and took off her hat, cloak and other parts of her dress, and disposed of them among the crowd, in despite of him. (The clothes in which criminals die are claimed as the perquisite of the executioner, unless a full equivalent is given him by the friends of the deceased.)
After much resistance he got the rope about her neck, which she had no sooner found accomplished, than, pulling a handkerchief, bound round her head, over her face, she threw herself out of the cart, before the signal given, with such violence, that she broke her neck, and died instantly, on the 4th of May, 1763.

Sometimes the executioners had troubles of their own, and ended where they had seen so many others.

The office of public executioner becoming vacant, it was given to Price, who, but for his extravagance, might have long continued in it, and subsisted on its dreadfully-earned wages. On returning from an execution, in the cart which had delivered some criminals into his hands, he was arrested in Holborn for debt, which he discharged, in part, with the wages he had that day earned, and the remainder from the produce of three suits of clothes, which he had taken from the bodies of the executed men. Not long afterwards he was lodged in the Marshalsea prison for other debts, and there remained for want of bail; in consequence whereof, being unable to attend his business at the next sessions of the Old Bailey, one William Marvel was appointed in his stead.
Having continued some time longer in the Marshalsea, he and a fellow-prisoner broke a hole in the wall,

through which they made their escape; and soon after this Price committed the horrid murder for which his life paid the forfeit.

John Price was indicted at the Old Bailey on the 24th of April, 1718, for the murder of Elizabeth, the wife of William White, on the 13th of the preceding month. In the course of the evidence it appeared that Price met the deceased near ten at night in Moorfields, and attempted to ravish her; but the poor woman (who was the wife of a watchman, and sold gingerbread in the streets) doing all in her power to resist his villainous attacks, he beat her so cruelly that streams of blood issued from her eyes and mouth, one of her arms was broken, some of her teeth knocked out, her head bruised in a most dreadful manner, one of her eyes forced from the socket; and he otherwise so ill treated her that the language of decency cannot describe it. Some persons, hearing the cries of the unhappy creature, repaired to the spot, took Price into custody, and lodged him in the watch-house; then conveyed the woman to a house, where a surgeon and nurse were sent for to attend her. Being unable to speak, she answered the nurse's questions by signs, and in that manner described what had happened to her. She died, after having languished four days.

The prisoner, on his trial, denied being guilty of the fact; and said that, as he was crossing Moorfields, he found something lying in his way; that he kicked at it, but discovered that it was a woman: he lifted her up, but she could not stand on her legs; and he said that he was taken into custody while he was thus employed. This defence, however, could not be credited, from what some former evidences had sworn; and the jury did not hesitate to find him guilty.

After sentence of death was passed on him, he abandoned himself to the drinking of spirituous liquors to such a degree as rendered him totally incapable of all the exercises of devotion. He obstinately denied the fact till the day of his execution, when he confessed that he had been guilty of it; but said that the crime was perpetrated when he was in a state of intoxication. He was executed in Bunhill-fields, on the 31st of May 1718, and, in his last moments, begged the prayers of the multitude, and hoped they would take warning by his untimely end. He was afterwards hung in chains near Holloway.

The last moments of some criminals, from the publicity of the execution, were inclined to have an air of peculiar levity. Such must have been the case when the sheriffs of London waved 'a final adieu' to the brothers Perreau, who 'bowed respectfully' to the sheriffs before being 'launched into eternity'.

On the day of the execution the brothers were favoured with a mourning-coach, and it was thought that thirty thousand people attended. They were both dressed in mourning, and behaved with the most Christian resolution. When they quitted the coach, and got into the cart, they bowed respectfully to the sheriffs, who waved their hands as a final adieu.

After the customary devotions, they crossed their hands, joining the four together, and in this manner were launched into eternity. They had not hung more than half a minute when their hands dropped asunder, and they appeared to die without pain.

The same gentlemanly demeanour was exhibited by Thomas Reeves, a footpad.

As they were going to execution the Ordinary asked Reeves if his wife had been concerned with him in any robberies. 'No,' said he; 'she is a worthy woman, whose first husband happening to be hanged, I married her, that she might not reproach me by a repetition of his virtues.'

Death had a natural fascination for humanity, because all were bound to suffer it and could never be

DRY BLOOD AND DISTANT THUNDER

told what it would be like. Selwyn's morbid interest was shared by the kindest of people, like Boswell and Reynolds, or by the most sensitive, like Byron. The latter went to a beheading in 1817, and expressed in a letter what was probably felt by the majority of spectators throughout the Age of Scandal.

The day before I left Rome I saw three robbers guillotined. The ceremony — including the *masqued* priests; the half-naked executioners; the bandaged criminals; the black Christ and his banner; the scaffold; the soldiery; the slow procession, and the quick rattle and heavy fall of the axe; the splash of the blood, and the ghastliness of the exposed heads — is altogether more impressive than the vulgar and ungentlemanly dirty 'new drop', and dog-like agony of infliction upon the sufferers of the English sentence. Two of these men behaved calmly enough, but the first of the three died with great terror and reluctance, which was very horrible. He would not lie down; then his neck was too large for the aperture, and the priest was obliged to drown his exclamations by still louder exhortations. The head was off before the eye could trace the blow; but from an attempt to draw back the head, notwithstanding it was held forward by the hair, the first head was cut off close to the ears: the other two were taken off more cleanly. It is better than the oriental way, and (I should think) than the axe of our ancestors. The pain seems little; and yet the effect to the spectator, and the preparation to the criminal, are very striking and chilling. The first turned me quite hot and thirsty, and made me shake so that I could hardly hold the opera-glass (I was close, but determined to see, as one should see everything, once, with attention); the second and third (which shows how dreadfully soon things grow indifferent), I am ashamed to say, had no effect on me as a horror, though I would have saved them if I could.

CHAPTER SIX

Backwaters

B<small>UT</small> while the *beau monde* was busy with its *agrémens*; while the prelates and politicians jockeyed for preferment and the world of literature dreamed about sultans, druids, incest or Gothick ruins; while the Mob drank itself blind for twopence on gin and the scientists, like Strulbugs in Swift, devoted themselves to the latest gossip about 'natural history', about the proceedings of the Royal Society, about chronometers, latitude and longitude, or about a prodigious telescope which the royal family could walk through without bumping the head; while music was a feud between Italy and Handel, and 'art' was the province of the virtuoso who had made the Grand Tour — Gibbon mentioned in 1785 that more than 40,000 English, masters and servants, were upon the Continent — while 'mistresses' were all but respectable and universities were given over to potations under the decayed remnants of medieval curricula; while the now eccentric flavours of the Age of Scandal were in a full bouquet, such as press-gangs, masquerades at Mrs. Cornelys' or at the Pantheon, gibbets, highwaymen, lap-dogs, disciples, weepers, diarists, watering-places, umbrellas known as 'Robinsons' after Robinson Crusoe, flagellants, takers of James's Powders, balloonists, duelists, pugilists, bootikins and Birthdays with a capital letter: while all these things were pushing down the main-stream of history with picturesque but per-

RURAL SCENE

haps with superficial charm, the quiet, deeper and perennial backwaters of that old England — whose population was less than nine million — continued, as they always had continued, and much as they do continue today.

Country life has survived in Britain with continuity, has survived the collapse of open-field cultivation, the troubles of enclosure and the Industrial Revolution, so that farmers will still repeat the agricultural saws of the Middle Ages and the village parson will still be a local potentate, as his ancestor the priest was, before the Reformation.

It was common in country districts [says Lecky] for a Sunday suit to descend from father to son. It was put on when the church bell rang and carefully put aside when the service had concluded, and in this way dresses of far bygone generations were still in actual use. Many years after the middle of the eighteenth century, it was stated that beaver hats made in the reign of Charles II, might be often seen in the village churches.

The quiet of the countryside, with its routine of husbandry in which the events are those of the weather, the procreation of cattle, or the different varieties of exhaustion which send the hind to his early bed for early rising, this remains as a constant from one 'period' to another, the backbone of everything defined as English. In the Age of Scandal it was perhaps the Woodforde diaries, more than the later roars of Cobbett or the cross remarks of William Cole, which conveyed the essence of the rustic scene. In five strong volumes of about four hundred pages each, and even then much abridged, the neat, particular handwriting of the eighteenth-century vicar is reproduced in print — with nothing whatever for him to say, and yet with a simple interest, in its way as gripping as if the narrative concerned the affairs of princes. It does, in fact, concern itself with nothing more exciting than the collection of tithes, the gravidity of maidservants, the dishes for dinner, an occasional jaunt to Bath or to the West Country, the archidiaconal visitations, the news of the family, the local gossip and the ailments of the diarist. It is written with brief, unimaginative meiosis. There is no self-examination; indeed, there is little examination of anything. The vicar's only love affair, an unsuccessful one, is related in half a dozen sentences, spaced over long intervals. The discharge of a blunderbuss is an event.

Jan 15, 1780. This being our gracious Queen Charlotte's Birth Day I fired my Blunderbuss with 3 Charges of Powder in it and a good deal of Paper, — and gave 3 Cheers.

The Reverend James Woodforde was born in 1740, of a long family of parsons; he was educated at Winchester and at New College, Oxford, where, like undergraduates of all periods, he sowed a few of his innocent wild oats:

June 14 (1761) ... Hearst, Bell and myself, being in Beer, went under Whitmore's window, and abused him very much, as being Dean, he came down, and sent us to our Proper Rooms, and then we Huzza'd him again and again. We are to wait on him tomorrow.

June 15. We waited on Whitmore this morning and he read to us a Statute or two and says he shall not mention again provided the Senr. People do not. I am to read the three first Books of Hutchinson's Moral Philosophy, and I am to give a summary account of them when I am examined for my Degree. . . .

Woodforde obtained a fellowship at his college, took holy orders, and, after a few years in the West Country and as a Proctor at Oxford, was given the college living at Weston in Norfolk, where he remained from 1774 until his death, unmarried, in 1803. He was a kindly proctor, and had early taken a resolution about his own drinking, which he kept, more or less, throughout life:

Septem. 7 [1763] . . . Had three bottles of Wine out of my room in ye B.C.R. this afternoon and Waring had another, out of his room. Waring was very drunk and Bedford was but little better. N.B. I was very sober, as I had made a resolution never to get drunk again, when at Geree's rooms in April last, when I fell down dead, and cut my Occiput very bad indeed.

He also had made a resolution against eating, which, it is to be feared, he did not keep so well:

Aug. 18 [1764] . . . I have made a promise today concerning a certain thing (in eating); which every time I break that promise I pay — 1 − 0.

The life at Weston Vicarage, during his thirty years of incumbency, was the life of most parsons. The study fire would smoke when the wind was in the W.S.W.; the chamber-pots would freeze in severe weather; a monstrous cheese would arrive as a present, with the Royal Arms stamped on the side; Mrs. Custance, the squire's wife, would produce a baby every year; some of these would live, some die, but always with a fee for the clergyman, wrapped genteelly in clean paper, for the christening or for the funeral.

The alarms and excursions of village life were the same as they are to the present day. Sometimes, indeed generally, the maidservants would get into trouble:

Nov. 6 [1778] ... This morning I had some suspicion that Bill was concerned with my Maid Nancy and also that she appeared to me to be with child. I was uneasy. But the truth will appear e'er long if so. Sukey my late Maid was at my House all day today to shew Nann to make Butter, and help in ironing. ...

Nov. 21 ... I told my Maid Betty this morning that the other maid Nancy looked so big about the Waist that I was afraid she was with Child, but Betty told me she thought not, but would soon inform me if it is so. ...

Nov. 23 ... I told Bill this morning that I should have nothing more to say to him or do for him — and I gave him his money that he desired me to keep for him. He was very low on the Occasion and cried much. ...

The menservants, unable to have babies, would tease the vicar by getting drunk:

Decem. 12 [1790] ... Lent my Servant Man, Ben Leggat, this Morning my Mare Phyllis to go to a Place called Crownthorpe on some particular Business of his own and he stayed out the whole day and was not returned home when I went to bed which was not till after one o'clock in the Morning. It made me and the whole Family very uneasy, thinking some Accident must have befallen him. It made me quite unhappy.

Decem. 13, Monday ... When I came down Stairs this Morning could hear no tidings of Ben at all, which still made me more uneasy. I then sent for Willm. Large and sent him on horseback after him. And about 2 o'clock Ben with Willm. Large returned and I thank God safe and well. Ben went Yesterday in the Afternoon with a Mr. Watson Steward to Sr. John Woodhouse to Kimberly Hall, where having made too free with the Baronets strong Beer, fell of his Horse coming home and lost her, so that he walked about all Night after her and did not find her till about Noon, she was found at Kimberley in a Stable of Mr. Hares, a boy happening to see and put her in there. I ordered Willm. Large to dine here and to have 2^s/0^d. Thank God! that Matters turned out no worse ... I was very indifferent all day long could eat but very little and not relish that, tho' we had a fine fat rost Goose for Dinner.

Sometimes even the pigs took it into their heads to behave disreputably.

April 15. [1778] ... We breakfasted, dined, supped and slept again at home. Brewed a vessell of strong Beer today. My two large Piggs, by drinking some Beer grounds taking out of one of my Barrels today, got so amazingly drunk by it, that they were not able to stand and appeared like dead things almost, and so remained all night from dinner time today. I never saw Piggs so drunk in my life, I slit their ears for them without feeling.

April 16. We breakfasted, dined supped and slept again at home. My 2 Piggs are still unable to walk yet, but they are better than they were yesterday. They tumble about the yard and can by no means stand at all steady yet. In the afternoon my 2 Piggs were tolerably sober.

Apart from these and similar immoralities, there were the petty accidents of life. A mysterious man would be found lurking in the earth closet at the end of the garden — Woodforde called it by the name of 'jericho' — who was obviously up to no good. The smuggler from whom the vicar obtained his spirits would be reported to the authorities, thus making it necessary to bury illicit kegs of rum. The gay young nieces would make an Apple Pye Bed. Mrs. Clarke, whose Constitution was very tender, would be taken in a Hysteric Fit while playing at Quadrille, but after taking Rhubarb at bed-time would be none the worse of it. 'Mrs. Davy fell downstairs but did not hurt herself. Miss Donne swallowed a Barley corn with its stalk. Many accidents happened but none very bad.' The maids who were not having babies would have convulsions. 'My Servant Maid Nanny Golding had another Fit this morning, screamed out most hideously and so loud that Ben heard her in a Field beyond the Cover, where he was hoeing Turnips. I never heard so frightful a Shriek or crying out. She continued in the fit near an Hour and then went to bed with a violent headache, and there lay all Day and night. It frightned us all. I must part with her at Michaelmas.' Dogs went mad. The labouring men would cut off their thumbs with sickles. 'It bled very much I put some Friars Balsam to it and had it bound up, he almost fainted.' The cow Polly would suffer from complicated disorders.

Feb. 3, Wednesday . . . My Cow Polly taken very bad in Calving this even' obliged to send to Johnny Reeve who stayed till near 12 o'clock at Night. She had a Calf at last but very bad after. Had 2 tubbs of Gin 5 Gallons each brought this evening to my House. Mrs. Custance took our Ladies out an Airing this Morn'.

Feb. 4, Thursday . . . My poor Cow very weak indeed not able to get up. . . .

Feb. 5, Friday . . . My poor Cow rather better this morning, but not able to get up as yet, she having a Disorder which I never heard of before or any of our Somersett Friends. It is called tail-shot, that is, a separation of some of the joints of the tail about a foot from the tip of the tail, or rather a slipping of one joint from another. It also makes all her teeth quite loose in her head. The Cure, is to open that part of the tail so slipt lengthways and put in an Onion boiled and some Salt, and bind it up with some coarse tape. . . .

The even tenor of life in Norfolk was far from being typified by these purple passages. For the most part it was a catalogue of coursing and fishing; of the records achieved by barometer or thermometer; of marriages, christenings, churchings and burials; of violent winds which terrified the vicar; or of crops and rain and prodigious dinners.

We had for Dinner 2 Dishes of soals fryed, Ham and 3 boiled chicken, a large piece of boiled Beef, Beans, a Couple of Ducks rosted and Peas, Gooseberry Pies and Currant Tarts. Our Desert after Dinner was, Rasberries, Strawberries, Gooseberries, and Currants, Almonds and Raisins, and a Couple of fine Melons — Mr. Jeans brought us a Melon in his Pocket. Port Wine and Mountain, strong Beer, Porter and Table Beer. They stayed with us till after 8 o'clock. Recd. for Butter this evening at 8d. 0.1.8.

It would be misleading to choose exciting snippets from Woodforde's diary, because its flavour was a singular one: it was the absorbing interest of boredom, and the emphasis of meiosis. For forty-five years,

THE SCANDALMONGER

from day to day, the round of visits and of little family affairs went on. People appeared and disappeared casually: sometimes with miniature drama, as was the case with the bibulous brother John or with the thoroughly untrustworthy Mr. Walker; sometimes with no apparent rhyme or reason, as is still the case with most of the affairs of man. Here, however, are a few extracts:

Oct. 26 [1768]. I had a poor little cat, that had one of her ribs broke and that laid across her belly, and we could not tell what it was, and she was in great pain. I therefore with a small pen knife this morning, opened one side of her and took it out, and performed the operation very well, and afterwards sewed it up and put Friars Balsam to it, and she was much better after, the incision was half an inch. It grieved me much to see the poor creature in such pain before, and therefore made me undertake the above, which I hope will preserve the life of the poor creature.

May 22 [1774] ... Have been very naughty today, did not go to either Ansford or Cary Church ... Have mercy on me O Lord a miserable, vile sinner, and pardon my failings.

Oct. 15 [1774] ... I caught a remarkable large Spider in my Wash Place this morning and put him in a small glass decanter and fed him with some bread and intend keeping him. ...

Jan. 25 [1779] ... Busy this morning in cleaning my Jack,[1] and did it completely. My stomach rather sick this evening — Mince Pye rose oft.

Mar. 23 [1779]. I breakfasted, and slept again at home. Memorandum. In shaving my face this morning I happened to cut one of my moles which bled

[1] Jericho.

much, and happening also to kill a small moth that was flying about, I applied it to my mole and it instantaneously stopped the bleeding.

Sept. 25 [1779] ... Mem: On Monday morn' last about 11 o'clock I pulled of the head of a large Flesh Fly, and the Body had life in it and stood upon his legs, and at different times moved his legs, and so continued till Thursday last, and then fell down. ...

Mar. 11, Friday (1791) ... Mem. The Stiony on my right Eye-lid still swelled and inflamed very much. As it is commonly said that the Eye-lid being rubbed by the tail of a black Cat would do it much good if not entirely cure it, and having a black Cat, a little before dinner I made a trial of it, and very soon after dinner I found my Eye-lid much abated of the swelling and almost free from Pain. I cannot therefore but conclude it to be of the greatest service to a Stiony on the Eye-lid. Any other Cats Tail may have the above effect in all probability — but I did my Eye-lid with my own black Tom Cat's Tail. ...

Mar. 12 ... My Eye much better, thank God for it.
Mar. 13 ... My Eye Lid still rather inflamed.
Mar. 14 ... My Eye Lid still poorly.
Mar. 15 ... My right Eye again, that is, its Eye-lid much inflamed again and rather painful. I put on a plaistor to it this morning, but in the Aft. took it of again, as I perceived no good from it. ...
Mar. 16, Wednesday ... My Eye-lid is I think rather better than it was, I bathed it with warm milk and Water last Night. I took a little Rhubarb going to bed to night. My Eye-lid about Noon rather worse owing perhaps to the warm Milk and Water, therefore just before Dinner I washed it well with cold Water and in the Evening appeared much better for it. ...
Mar. 17, Thursday ... My Eye-lid much better today, washed it well with cold Water this Morning. ...
Mar. 18, Friday ... My Eye-lid much better indeed to day by often patting it with cold Water.

THE SCANDALMONGER

Mar. 19, Saturday . . . My Eye-lid almost entirely well (thank God) to day.

It would be impossible to quote from the common life of this diarist *in extenso* without quoting five volumes. In the three following consecutive entries, perhaps there may be found a microcosm of it. The baby to which he refers appears, dies and is buried, in a setting of farm prices and dinner menus, and this, perhaps, was the average experience of a kind, timid, precise and charmingly unsuccessful eighteenth-century country cleric.

Oct. 18, Tuesday (1791) . . . I privately baptized this morning at my House a Child of William Burnhams by name Sarah. . . .

Oct. 19, Wednesday . . . Mr. Girling called on me this Morning and paid me for five Coomb of Oats which Mr. Custance had of me the 11. of June last at $10^s/0^d$, 2.10.0. Mr. Forster of Lenewade Bridge sent me this Morning a dozen fine Eels. The Infant I baptized Yesterday Morn died last Night — I thought it could not live, it looked so black. It is I hope an happy release for it. It is to be buried to Morrow. Dinner to day, Eels and a fine Piece of Rost Beef.

Oct. 20, Thursday . . . About one o'clock this Afternoon I walked to Weston-Church and buried Sarah Burnham the Infant I baptized tuesday last, aged 3 Days. Dinner to day, Eels and a Leg Mutton rosted.

CHAPTER SEVEN

Eccentrics

It may have been due to their bad teeth or to their rotten tonsils, before these forms of poisoning had been identified; or it may have been due to the quantities of alcohol consumed by many; or perhaps the root may have been podagral: whatever the explanation, the incidence of lunacy in the second half of the eighteenth century seems to have been high. Not only was the King himself a manic-depressive, but his first minister also, the elder Pitt, suffered during great part of his administration from a toxic condition which produced the attitudes of melancholia.

Lord Chatham's state of health [wrote Mr. Whateley] is certainly the lowest dejection and debility that mind or body can be in. He sits all day leaning on his hands, which he supports on the table; does not permit any person to remain in the room; knocks when he wants anything; and having made his wants known, gives a signal, without speaking, to the person who answered his call to retire.

His sickly and uncertain appetite [wrote Walpole] was never regular, and his temper could put up with no defect: thence a succession of chickens were boiling and roasting at every hour, to be ready whenever he should call.

It was not only the politicians and the kings who suffered from imbecility — there were lunatic monarchs in Prussia, Russia, Denmark, Portugal and perhaps elsewhere — but also the peerage and the landed gentry. Dukes like he of Bolton might suddenly sit on the floor and blow their brains out, causing Walpole to observe:

The Duke of Bolton the other morning — nobody knows why or wherefore, except that there is a good deal of madness in the blood, sat himself down upon the floor of his dressing-room, and shot himself through the head. What is more remarkable is, that it is the same house and the same chamber in which Lord Scarborough performed the same exploit. I do not believe that shooting oneself through the head is catching.

Earls like Ferrers might send for their stewards and shoot them down. Horace Walpole's own nephew, Lord Orford, who spent much of his life insane, would

do nothing but speak in the lowest voice, and would whisper to them at the length of the table, when the person next to him could not distinguish what he said. Every evening, precisely at the same hour, sitting round a table, he would join his forehead to his mistress's (who is forty, red-faced, and with black teeth, and with whom he has lived these twenty years), and there they would sit for a quarter of an hour, like two parroquets, without speaking.

The Townshend family, more metaphysical, would get into an argument about Life with a capital letter, with fatal results:

This boy [Lord William Townshend] from infancy had a tendency to insanity. Some years after his being in India, he was travelling in England with one of his brothers in a postchaise, when their conversation was whether life under all the evils that attended it was

ECCENTRICS

worth keeping? After a long discussion they were both of opinion that the evils so greatly outweighed the blessings that existence was not desirable: they therefore immediately determined to withdraw themselves from it, and taking out a pair of pistols they had in the carriage they intended each to shoot the other, or each to shoot himself. It was never ascertained which was the fact; one shot took effect, proving fatal instantaneously, I do not recollect upon which of them; the other pistol missed fire. The postilion stopping upon hearing the report, got off his horse and opening the door of the carriage found one of them fallen off his seat, weltering in his blood, the other sitting very composedly. Upon being asked what had happened to his brother he made no answer, nor would he even state a single circumstance relative to the transaction. He has ever since been confined as a lunatic.

WILLIAM HICKEY

In the republic of literature, moreover, there was scarcely a man who claimed to be of sound mind. Cowper, Smart, Gray, Johnson, Boswell, Blake and Lamb, all owned to the soft impeachment of mental affliction, sometimes homicidal, sometimes not.

Perhaps it was a sign of the times. Perhaps so eccentric a century was bound to have an abundance of examples, slightly more eccentric than the rest.

There was the odd Duke of Queensberry, whose effect upon the London milk supply has been noted in the first volume. Born in 1725, and devoted to betting, to Newmarket or to 'splendid vice, of almost oriental voluptuousness', it was he who 'performed, in his own drawing-room, the scene of Paris and the goddesses. Three of the most beautiful females in London presented themselves before him, precisely as

THE SCANDALMONGER

the divinities of Homer are supposed to have appeared to Paris on Mount Ida: while *he*, habited like the Dardan shepherd, holding a gilded apple in his hand, conferred the prize on her whom he deemed the fairest.' In old age, according to Jesse, 'in fine sunny weather, it was the custom of the Duke of Queensberry to seat himself in his balcony in Piccadilly, where his figure was familiar to every person who was in the habit of passing through the great thoroughfare. Here (his emaciated figure, rendered the more conspicuous from his custom of holding a parasol over his head), he was in the habit of watching every attractive form, and ogling every pretty face that met his eye. He is said, indeed, to have kept a pony and servant in constant readiness, in order to follow, and ascertain the residence of any fair girl whose attractions particularly caught his fancy.' The duke retained a doctor, whom he only paid when he was well, and died 'with great firmness' in 1810, at the age of eighty-six, his death-bed being strewed 'with billets and letters to the number of at least seventy, mostly, indeed, addressed to him by females of every description and of every rank, from duchesses down to ladies of the easiest virtue. Unable, from his extenuated state, to open or to peruse them he ordered them as they arrived to be laid on his bed, where they remained, the seals unbroken, till he expired' — unmarried.

There was the Chevalier d'Eon, the fencer and diplomat, who spent the first half of his life in breeches and the second half in petticoats. Hannah More met him in the latter garment:

On Friday I gratified the curiosity of many years, by meeting at dinner Madame la Chevalière d'Eon: she is extremely entertaining, has universal information, wit, vivacity, and gaiety. Something too much of the latter, (I have heard) when she has taken a bottle or two of Burgundy; but this being a very sober party, she was kept entirely within the limits of decorum. General Johnson was of the party, and it was ridiculous to hear her military conversation. Sometimes it was, 'Quand j'étais colonel d'un tel regiment!' then again, 'Non, c'était quand j'étais secrétaire d'ambassade du Duc de Nivernois,' or 'Quand je négociais la paix de Paris.' She is, to be sure, a phenomenon in history; and, as such, a great curiosity. But *one* d'Eon is enough, and *one slice* of her quite sufficient.

Walpole met the Chevalier in both forms, but was more amused by the feminine one:

I received a little Italian note from Mrs. Cosway, this morning, to tell me that, as I had at her house last week met an old acquaintance, without knowing her, I might meet her again this evening, *en connoissance de cause*, as Mademoiselle la Chevalière d'Eon, who, as Mrs. Cosway told me, had taken it ill that I had not reconnoitred her, and said she must be strangely altered — the devil is in it, if she is not! — but alack! I have found her altered again; adieu to the abbatical dignity that I had fancied I discovered; I now found her loud, noisy, and vulgar; indeed, I believe she had dined a little *en dragon*. The night was hot, she had no muff or gloves, and her hands and arms seem not to have participated of the change of sexes, but are fitter to carry a chair than a fan.

Lady Louvain wished to see Mademoiselle D'Eon [he wrote later], and Mr. Dutens invited her. The Lady asked her if she had ever been at Dijon, and said she herself had lain in there. 'I have been there,' said Miss Hector, 'but did not lie in there, *car je suis vierge, et pour que les vierges accouchent, il faut qu'elles aillent à Jerusalem.*' It was impertinent to Lady Louvain, and worse in a clergyman's house; but women of fashion should not go aboard Amazons.

She seems to have a noble, independent, as well as intrepid mind [wrote Anna Seward more kindly] — and the muscular strength and activity of her large frame at sixty-nine, are wonderful. She fences in the French uniform, and then appears an athletic, venerable, graceful man. In the female garb, as might be expected, she is awkwardly, though not vulgarly masculine.

Bets were laid on her sex, which were only decided at her death. Then Lady Jerningham wrote, in 1810:

It is a most extraordinary event. Père Elisé, who Called upon her every day during her illness, made his visit, about 2 hours after She had expired, and, going up to the Bed to Look at Her, and reflecting upon all the past Historys about Her, Lifted up the Sheet *Machinalement* and Screamed out to the dismay of the Femme de Chambre: *C'est un Homme!*

So far as mixed sexes went, there was a regular plethora of female soldiers in Walpole's century. Phoebe Hessel claimed to have been wounded at Fontenoy, and lived to be 108. Mother Ross of the 2nd Dragoons was buried among the Chelsea pensioners with three grand volleys over her grave. Hannah Snell, who was known to her comrades as 'hearty Jemmy', said that she had received five hundred lashes from the sergeant, and was wounded at Pondicherry. Mary Ann Talbot, the 'British Amazon', was both soldier, cabin-boy and powder-monkey but took to drink and ended as a domestic servant, though a tiresome one.

A major eccentric was Thomas Day, the author of *Sandford and Merton*, who, having been born in 1748

OLD Q ON THE BALCONY

CHEVALIER D'EON

and bitten with the madness of Rousseau, determined to educate a wife for himself. The story may be found in Hesketh Pearson's *Doctor Darwin*:

Among other things, he wanted his wife to be as 'simple as a mountain girl, in her dress, her diet, and her manners; fearless and intrepid as the Spartan wives and Roman heroines'..... .

With a barrister friend, Mr. Bicknel, he descended upon the town of Shrewsbury, and, armed with credentials of his moral probity, visited the Foundling Hospital there. From among the 'prattling inmates of that institution' (to quote Blackman) he selected a girl aged eleven — Anna Seward describes her as 'a clear, auburn brunette, with dark eyes, glowing bloom and chestnut tresses' — whom he called Sabrina Sidney. (She owed her Christian name to the River Severn and her surname to Day's hero, Algernon.) Day and Bicknel then visited the Foundling Hospital in London, where they selected another girl, aged twelve — described by Anna as 'fair, with flaxen locks and light eyes' — and called her Lucretia.

Day proposed to keep whichever of these turned out to be the better, and to give a dowry to the other. He took them to France, and, after two years of desperate trouble as a nursery maid, he started on the higher, the Stoic education.

There were, he decided, two classes of cowards — those who shrank from immediate physical pain, and those were were terrified by the apprehension of danger. His methods were carefully selected to prove complete immunity from cowardice in both forms, should the patient survive the ordeal. First, he believed that the dropping of melted sealing-wax on the neck and arms of Sabrina would, if she treated it as an ordinary occurrence, definitely signify her indifference to immediate physical pain. He tried it, but was disagreeably surprised to note that, as the wax sizzled and hardened on her flesh, she so far forgot herself as to scream.

But there was still hope. A woman who could not endure acute suffering, because of some inherited effeminacy, might yet be stoical under the threat of mortal danger. He informed her therefore that he had loaded his pistol and begged her to have sufficient faith in the accuracy of his aim, and his proved affection for herself, not to jump when he fired a bullet into her petticoats. Taking a careful aim at her legs, he then fired off a blank cartridge, and was shocked to observe that she not only jumped but emitted a howl of terror. He was not, however, callous enough to give her up in despair at the first failure. He wanted her to have every possible chance of gaining his good opinion; so he went on blazing away hopefully at her skirts . . . In the hope that hardening would come with time, he repeated these experiments, with others of a similar nature, at intervals during his year's residence at Lichfield; but Sabrina never really got used to them, and continually vexed him with her querulous complaints.

In the end, neither of the two young ladies proved to be acceptable as wives, and the enthusiast had to content himself with being painted by Wright of Derby. 'Drawn as in the open air, the surrounding sky is tempestuous, lurid and dark. He stands leaning his left arm against a column inscribed to Hampden. Mr. Day looks upward, as enthusiastically meditating on the contents of the book, held in his dropped right hand. The open leaf is the oration of that virtuous patriot in the senate, against the grant of ship-money, demanded by King Charles the First. A flash of lightning plays in Mr. Day's hair, and illuminates the contents of the volume.'

ECCENTRICS

Another oddity was Maria Edgeworth's father, who, according to Pearson,

kept several terms at the Temple, read scientific books, constructed a carriage, played cards, made experiments . . . Some of his inventions were more curious than useful. One was a sailing carriage, which threatened to distribute the horse traffic on the roads about Reading in a most alarming manner. Another was a giant wooden horse, which, by a strange arrangement of front and rear legs, could carry him safely over any wall in the country. He experimented on this at intervals for forty years, but never achieved complete success. A third was a huge hollow wheel, by walking within which a man could travel much faster than his legs could naturally take him. This interesting novelty was wrecked before completion by a small boy, who got into it and began to ply his legs. The wheel, helped by a gentle incline, needed no human encouragement and dashed off in the direction of a chalk-pit. The boy saved his life by jumping out, but the wheel refused to be saved and was picked up in small fragments the following morning by its sorrowful contriver, who had not enough capital to give the experiment a further trial.

There was Dr. Darwin himself, the grandfather of the biologist, who invented water-closets — or reinvented them — luminous music, speaking-machines, artificial birds and even a plan by which,

If the nations who inhabit this hemisphere of the globe, instead of destroying their seamen and exhausting their wealth in unnecessary wars, could be induced to unite their labours to navigate the immense masses of ice in the polar regions into the more southern seas, two great advantages would result to mankind; the tropic countries would be much cooled by their solution, and our winters in this latitude would

THE SCANDALMONGER

be rendered much milder for perhaps a century or two, till the masses of ice became again enormous.

In the year 1768 [wrote Anna Seward], Dr. Darwin met with an accident of irretrievable injury to the human frame. His propensity to mechanics had unfortunately led him to construct a very singular carriage. It was a platform, with a seat fixed upon a very high pair of wheels, and supported in the front, upon the back of the horse, by means of a kind of proboscis, which, forming an arch, reached over the hindquarters of the horse; and passed through a ring, placed on an upright piece of iron, which worked in a socket, fixed in the saddle. The horse could thus move from one side of the road to the other, quartering, as it is called, at the will of the driver, whose constant attention was necessarily employed to regulate a piece of machinery contrived, but *not well* contrived, for that purpose. From this whimsical carriage the doctor was several times thrown, and the last time he used it, had the misfortune, from a similar accident, to break the patella of his right knee, which caused, as it must always cause, an incurable weakness in the fractured part, and a lameness, not very discernible, indeed, when walking on even ground.

Apart from those who were mechanically afflicted, there were eccentric misers like the pleasant Elwes, a favourite of Horace Walpole's, whose one amusement was partridge-shooting, and who consequently had to live on partridges. Nollekens was so mean that he only owned one pair of small-clothes. Neild would not allow his clothes to be brushed because it destroyed the nap, but he left £500,000 to Queen Victoria. And Daniel Dancer, who bequeathed £3000 per annum, dressed mainly in hay-bands. The least sufferable of contemporary misers tried to cheapen

ECCENTRICS

his own daughter's funeral by pointing out that he had another daughter who would be dying soon, and that he would send her to the same undertaker.

The *Dictionary of National Biography* is embarrassed with a richness of oddities, flourishing in the Age of Scandal. The unusual vice-provost of Trinity College, Dublin, John Barrett (1752-1821), 'would sometimes go down to the kitchen to warm himself, but to this the servants objected on account of his dirty and ragged condition'. Jeremy Bentham (1748-1832) — whose skeleton in its original clothes is preserved at University College, London — invented what he called 'auto-icons'. Dead people were to be embalmed and used as their own monuments. 'If a country gentleman have rows of trees leading to his dwelling, the auto-icons of his family might alternate with the trees; copal varnish would protect the face from the effects of rain — caoutchouc the habiliments.' Nathaniel Bentley (1735-1809), known as Dirty Dick, refused to have his premises cleaned or dusted for forty years. The great philosopher and exponent of tar-water, Bishop Berkeley (1685-1753), 'induced his friend Contarini, Goldsmith's uncle, to hang him experimentally. He was cut down when nearly senseless, and exclaimed, "Bless my heart, Contarini, you have rumpled my band!"' Joseph Black (1728-99), an eminent and precise chemist, died with his accustomed precision. 'Being at table with his usual fare, some bread, a few prunes, and a measured quantity of milk diluted with water, and having the cup in his hand when the last stroke of the pulse was to be given, he appeared to have set it down on his knees, which were joined together, and in the action expired without spilling a drop, as if an experiment had been purposely made to evince the facility with which he departed.' The famous Ladies of Llangollen — Lady Eleanor Butler and Sarah Ponsonby — retired to Wales and lived in seclusion and semi-masculine costume. Chatterton's father could put his clenched fist in his mouth. Romeo Coates (1772-1848) drove round Bath in a carriage shaped like a kettle-drum 'and across the bar of his curricle was a large brazen cock, with this motto, "Whilst I live I'll crow." ' Cornwall, the Speaker of the House of Commons (1735-89), kept a replenished mug of beer in the House, and caused inconvenience by going to sleep from its effects. Patrick Cotter (1761-1806) was eccentric enough to be eight feet seven inches high — while Joseph Boruwlaski (1739-1837) was content with thirty-nine inches and lived to be nearly a hundred. Cracherode (1730-99), the timid bibliophile, held a manor of the King subject to the service of presenting a coronation cup, and the dread 'lest he should at any time be called upon to undertake this service embittered his life'. John Crofton the antiquary (1732-1820) read the whole of *Don Quixote* to his wife in Spanish, although she did not understand a word of that language. John Dalton (1766-1844), chemist and natural philosopher, ascended Helvellyn between thirty and forty times, and, when asked the reason why he had not married, replied, 'I never had time.' Daniel Day (1683-1767) 'left directions that his body should be conveyed to the grave by water, in consequence of the number of accidents he had met with while travelling on land, and that it should be accompanied by six pump-and-block makers'. John

ECCENTRICS

Deare the sculptor (1759-98) 'caught a fatal cold by sleeping on a block of marble of peculiar shape, expecting to get inspiration in his dreams for carving it'. Thomas Dermody the poet (1775-1802) 'abandoned himself to vice, saying, "I am vicious because I like it."' Robert Deverell, formerly Pedley (1760-1841), wrote a book to show that all the characters in Shakespeare were merely references to the moon. Lamb's friend George Dyer (1755-1841), on being told that a man called Williams had murdered two whole families, observed that Williams 'must have been rather an eccentric character'. An actor called John Edwin (1768-1805), who had received an adverse criticism, wrote to a friend, 'Come and help me to destroy myself with some of the most splendid cogniac [sic] that I have ever exported to cheer a breaking heart', and duly destroyed himself by that means. The Duke of Bridgewater (1736-1803) would talk of nothing but canals, rooted up all the flowers in his garden and would not allow any woman servant to wait upon him. The Earl of Bridgewater (1756-1829) had a house filled with cats and dogs, 'some of which were dressed up as men and women, and were driven out in his carriage, and fed at his table'. John Fransham the free-thinker (1730-1810) lived on a farthing's worth of potatoes a day, considered that to make his bed more than once a week was 'the height of effeminacy', thought dogs to be 'noisy, mobbish and vulgar', ate tarts till he got a headache in order to enjoy the contrasting pleasures of health, burned his hautboy to make tea, and 'supplying its place with a "bilbo-catch", he persevered until he had caught the ball on the spike 666,666 times (not in succession;

he could never exceed a sequence of two hundred)'. Lord Gardenstone (1721-93) had 'an extreme fondness for pigs', which he kept in his bedroom, explaining: 'It is just a bit sow, poor beast, and I laid my breeches on it to keep it warm all night.' James Graham (1745-94), the quack doctor who kept a not very respectable Temple of Health and Hymen visited by Horace Walpole, and who, incidentally, is said to have employed Nelson's Lady Hamilton there in her earlier years, was fond of 'earth-bathing'; and 'we are told that he and a young lady of Newcastle "stripped into their first suits", and were each interred up to the chin, their heads beautifully powdered and dressed, appearing not unlike two fine, full-grown cauliflowers'. From December 31st, 1792, to January 15th, 1793, 'he neither ate, drank nor took anything but cold water, sustaining life by wearing cut-up turfs against his naked body, and by rubbing his limbs with his own nervous aethereal balsam'. The mother of Thomas Greenhill (1681-1740) 'had by one husband thirty-nine children, all (it is said) born alive and baptised, and all single births except one'. John Henderson (1757-88) would go to bed at daybreak 'after putting on a shirt which he had made perfectly wet' at the pump. Orator Henley (1692-1756) invented a new way of making shoes — which was by cutting off the tops of boots. The eleventh Duke of Norfolk (1746-1815) was called 'Dirty Jockey of Norfolk', and could only be washed by his servants when drunk in bed. Hortensia, one of the favourite whores of Dr. Johnson (c. 1778), would 'walk up and down the Park, repeating a book of Virgil'. John Howell the polyartist (1788-1863) broke his leg trying

ECCENTRICS

to fly and 'having made at considerable expense, a model in the shape of a fish, he entered the machine, tried to swim under water at Leith, and was nearly drowned'. Henry Constantine Jennings (1731-1819), virtuoso, was believed to keep an oven in his house for the cremation of his body, and, on getting up in the morning, he 'mounted his chaise-horse, composed of leather and inflated like a pair of bellows, and took exactly one thousand gallops'. Richard Kirwan (1733-1812) lived on ham and milk. 'Flies were his especial aversion; he kept a pet eagle, and was attended by six large dogs.' Daniel Lambert (1770-1809) 'attained the acme of mortal hugeness'. He weighed $52\frac{3}{4}$ stone and his coffin was built upon two axle-trees and four wheels, being rolled down a gradual incline to the grave. Jane Lewson (1700-1816) would never allow water to be used in her house, for fear of catching cold, washed her hands with lard, and by these precautions lived to be about 116. John Metcalf (1717-1810), though totally blind, was a jockey, swimmer, soldier, gallant, horse-dealer, coach-conductor and road-maker, who surveyed and laid out 180 miles of road without assistance. John Mitford (1782-1831), having been 'discharged from the navy as insane', 'took to journalism and strong drink'. He lived for forty-three days in a gravel pit, with pen, ink and paper, being allowed a shilling a day by his publisher, of which he expended tenpence on gin and twopence on bread, cheese and an onion. Ann Moore (*fl.* 1813), the 'fasting woman of Tutbury', was believed to live on air. Beau Nash (1674-1761) was accustomed to make bets 'such as that he would ride through a village on cowback naked'. William Paley of the

THE SCANDALMONGER

Evidences (1743-1805) fell off his pony seven times on the road to Cambridge, 'his father only turning his head on such occasions to say, "Take care of thy money, lad." ' Sir Ralph Payne (1738-1807), governor of the Leeward Islands, 'was attended by an army of servants, but he would not allow any of the black servitors about him to wear shoes or stockings, their legs being rubbed daily with butter so that they shone like jet; and he would not, if he could avoid it, handle a letter or parcel from their fingers. To escape the indignity, he designed a golden instrument, like a tongs, with which he held any article which was given him by a black servant'. Robert Pigott (1736-94) 'fulminated against hats, arguing that they had been introduced by priests and despots, and that they concealed the face and were gloomy and monotonous'. Richard Pockrich (1690-1757) proposed 'to supply men-of-war with tin boats which would not sink, to secure immortality by the transfusion of blood, and to provide human beings with wings'. The first person to have a glass pane in his coffin seems to have been Robert Robinson, D.D. (1727-91), who also had an unlocked mausoleum and a watchman to see if he breathed on the glass. The only peer, perhaps the only gentleman of Great Britain, who wore a beard with his wig, was Lord Rokeby (1713-1800). He 'lived chiefly on beef-tea, and was an enthusiastic water-drinker. He abhorred fires, and had a bath so constructed as to be warmed only by the rays of the sun, and passed much of his time in it'. Sir Lumley Skeffington (1771-1850), a beau who was consulted on the subject of attire by Prinny and who invented a new colour called Skeffington Brown, maintained

ECCENTRICS

that the secret of life lay in never stirring out of doors during the cold, damp winter months. He was known as 'Skiffy Skipt-on', owing to his 'wonted grace'. The fourth Earl of Harrington (1780-1851) 'designed the Petersham overcoat and the Petersham snuff mixture, and mixed his own blacking... His hats were also peculiar'. Everybody knows that Lady Hester Stanhope (1776-1839), niece of the great Earl of Chatham, settled on Mount Lebanon as a female sheikh. Walking Stewart (1749-1822), a general of Hyder Ali's and prime minister to the Nabob of Arcot, covered most of the globe except China and Africa on foot, and at other times reposed in 'trance-like reverie among the cows of St. James's Park, inhaling their balmy breath and pursuing his philosophical speculations'. Benjamin Stillingfleet the naturalist (1702-71) was so modest that he always wrote of himself with a small 'i'. William Tatham (1752-1819) adopted an unusual mode of committing suicide, with a cannon. John Nicholas Thom (1799-1838) claimed first to be the Earl of Devon, later to be the King of Jerusalem, and finally to be the Messiah. A butcher called Samuel Thorley, according to the *Eccentric Mirror*, 'having frequently heard that human flesh resembled young pig in taste, curiosity prompted him to try if it was true'. He consequently butchered a ballad-singer named Ann Smith, cut her up, and sampled some of her boiled. She disagreed with him. 'During his imprisonment and trial he behaved with the greatest indifference, and at the gallows only inquired if the executioner intended to strip him; when receiving an answer in the negative, he displayed a slight degree of satisfaction.' The painter

THE SCANDALMONGER

Varley (1778-1842), a powerful man, kept his own horoscope day by day, boxed for refreshment and 'when tired of boxing, he and his pupils would toss Mrs. Varley from one to the other across the table'. The second Earl Verney (1712-91) escaped from his creditors in his wife's hearse.

It is unwise to laugh at one's ancestors, for all that, and the reader will have noted that various ideas of unsinkable lifeboats, blood transfusion, aircraft and submarines were mooted by the eccentrics of the Age of Scandal. The invention of the gramophone was by no means a monopoly of Edison's.

I promise to pay Dr. Darwin of Lichfield one thousand pounds upon his delivering to me (within two years of date hereof) an Instrument called an organ that is capable of pronouncing the Lord's prayer, the creed and ten Commandments in the vulgar tongue and his ceding to me and me only the property of the sd invention with all the advantages thereto appertaining.
M. BOULTON, Soho, Sep. 3rd 1777.
Witness: JAMES KEIR.
Witness: W. SMALL.

It was a dynamic age, through which there stalked the ghosts of great ideas: sometimes of real premonitions, some of them, perhaps, still to come. Jet-propulsion, of which we make such a fuss today, was invented by George Medhurst (1759-1827), whose 'Aeolian Engine' was to drive carriages on common roads by compressed air in a reservoir under the vehicle. Rocket-bombs were known to Wellington. A mysterious New Weapon, no bigger than a duck-egg, was invented by Samuel Warner (d. 1853), which was said to have utterly destroyed two French privateers with all hands; but, as the Admiralty would not pay him the £200,000 which he demanded, and as he would not reveal the secret without the money, it sank into oblivion. Perhaps the oddest of contemporary mysteries was the 'secret war plan' of Admiral Cochrane (1775-1860). The nature of this 'was never made public, though he repeatedly declared that it was capable of destroying any fleet or fortress in the world. He first proposed it as early as 1811, when it was referred to a secret committee, consisting of the Duke of York, Lord Keith, Lord Exmouth, and the two Congreves, who pronounced it to be infallible, irresistible, but inhuman. On this ground it was not adopted; but when the inventor entered the service of Chili he was pledged by the Prince Regent not to use it for any other country than his own'. Cochrane ended as the Earl of Dundonald. 'After his re-admission to the English navy this secret plan was several times urged on the Admiralty and the government, and was brought prominently into notice during the Russian War of 1854-56; but on every occasion it was put on one side as too terrible and inhuman, though always with the clear admission that it was capable of producing the results which Dundonald claimed for it.'

Perhaps it was appropriate to the eccentricity of the era that the only authentic instance of a prophetic vision should have visited a gentleman who was born in 1753. John Williams, a banker, on May 2nd or 3rd, 1812, dreamed three times in one night that he saw a man shot in the lobby of the House of Commons, with which he was familiar, and he was informed in his dream that the victim was Mr. Spencer Perceval. On

May 4th he actually consulted his business partners on the propriety of warning the Prime Minister. He was dissuaded from doing so. On May 11th, Perceval was shot by the lunatic Bellingham, under all the circumstances of a successful Experiment with Time.

CHAPTER EIGHT

An Early Surrealist

'THE Prince of Palagonia,' writes Brydone in his *Tour through Sicily and Malta*, 'a man of immense fortune, has devoted his whole life to the study of monsters and chimeras, greater and more ridiculous than ever entered into the imagination of the wildest writers of romance or knight-errantry.

'The amazing crowd of statues that surround his house, appear at a distance like a little army drawn up for its defence; but when you get amongst them, and every one assumes his true likeness, you may imagine you have got into the regions of delusion and enchantment; for of all that immense group, there is not one made to represent any object in nature; nor is the absurdity of the wretched imagination that created them less astonishing than its wonderful fertility. It would require a volume to describe the whole, and a sad volume indeed it would make. He has put the heads of men to the bodies of every sort of animal, and the heads of every other animal to the bodies of men. Sometimes he makes a compound of five or six animals that have no sort of resemblance in nature. He puts the head of a lion to the neck of a goose, the body of a lizard, the legs of a goat, the tail of a fox. On the back of this monster he puts another, if possible, still more hideous, with five or six heads, and a bush of horns, that beats the beast in the Revelations all to nothing. There is no kind of horn

THE SCANDALMONGER

in the world that he has not collected; and his pleasure is to see them all flourishing on the same head. It would be idle and tiresome to be particular in an account of these absurdities. The statues that adorn, or rather deform, the great avenue, and surround the court of the palace, amount already to six hundred, notwithstanding which, it may be truly said, that he has not broken the second commandment; for of all that number, there is not the likeness of anything in heaven above, in the earth beneath, or in the waters under the earth. The old ornaments which were put up by his father, who was a sensible man, appear to have been in good taste. They have all been knocked to pieces, and laid together in a heap, to make room for this new creation.

'The inside of this enchanted castle corresponds exactly with the out; it is in every respect as whimsical and fantastical, and you cannot turn yourself to any side, where you are not stared in the face by some hideous figure or other. Some of the apartments are spacious and magnificent, with high arched roofs; which, instead of plaster or stucco, are composed entirely of large mirrors, nicely joined together. The effect that these produce (as each of them makes a small angle with the other) is exactly that of a multiplying glass; so that when three or four people are walking below, there is always the appearance of three or four hundred walking above. The whole of the doors are likewise covered over with small pieces of mirror, cut into the most ridiculous shapes, and intermixed with a great variety of crystal and glass of different colours. All the chimney-pieces, windows, and side-boards, are crowded with pyramids and

SCENE IN BEDLAM

AN EARLY SURREALIST

pillars of tea-pots, candle-cups, bowls, cups, saucers, &c., strongly cemented together; some of these columns are not without their beauty: one of them has a large china chamber-pot for its base, and a circle of pretty little flower-pots for its capital: the shaft of the column, upwards of four feet long, is entirely composed of tea-pots of different sizes, diminished gradually from the base to the capital. The profusion of China that has been employed in forming these columns is incredible: there are not less than forty pillars and pyramids formed in this strange fantastic manner. — Most of the rooms are paved with fine marble tables of different colors, that look like so many tombstones, some of these are richly wrought with lapis lazuli, porphyry, and other valuable stones; their fine polish is now gone, and they only appear like common marble; the place of these beautiful tables he has supplied by a new set of his own invention, some of which are not without their merit. These are made of the finest tortoise-shell mixed with mother-of-pearl, ivory, and a variety of metals; and are mounted on fine stands of solid brass.

'The windows of this enchanted castle are composed of a variety of glass of every different colour, mixed without any sort of order or regularity, blue, red, green, yellow, purple, violet. The house-clock is cased in the body of a statue; the eyes of the figure move with the pendulum, turning up their white and black alternately, and make a hideous appearance.

'His bed-chamber and dressing-room are like two appartments in Noah's ark; there is scarcely a beast, however vile, that he has not placed there; toads, frogs, serpents, lizards, scorpions, all cut out in marble, of their respective colours. There are a good many busts, too, that are not less singularly imagined. — Some of these make a very handsome profile on one side; turn to the other, and you have a skeleton; here you see a nurse with a child in her arms; its back is exactly that of an infant, its face is that of a wrinkled old woman of ninety.

'The family statues are charming; they have been done from some old pictures; and make a most venerable appearance; he has dressed them out from head to foot in new and elegant suits of marble; and indeed the effect it produces is more ridiculous than anything you can conceive. Their shoes are all of black marble, their stockings generally red; their clothes are of different colours, blue, green and variegated, with a rich old-fashioned lace. The periwigs of the men and head-dresses of the ladies are of fine white; so are their shirts, with long flowing ruffles of alabaster.

'The author and owner of this singular collection is a poor miserable lean figure, shivering at a breeze, and seems to be afraid of everybody he speaks to. He is one of the richest subjects in the island, and it is thought he has not laid out less than 20,000 l., in the creation of this world of monsters and chimeras. — He certainly might have fallen upon some way to prove himself a fool at a cheaper rate. However, it gives bread to a number of poor people, to whom he is an excellent master. His house at Palermo is a good deal in the same style; his carriages are covered with plates of brass, so that some of them are musquet-proof.

'The government have had serious thoughts of demolishing the regiment of monsters he has placed around his house; but as he is humane and inoffensive, and as this would certainly break his heart, they have as yet forborne. However, the seeing of them by women with child is said to have been attended with very unfortunate circumstances; and ladies complain that they dare no longer take an airing in the Bagaria; that some hideous form always haunts their imagination for some time after; their husbands, too, it is said, are as little satisfied with the great variety of horns.'

CHAPTER NINE

A Private Paestum

No excursion through the avenues of the late eighteenth century would be complete without a visit to one of its palaces — to one of those vast country houses like Stowe or Blenheim, which could only be afforded by half a dozen subjects in the kingdom, but which were the centre of hospitality for many.

I have been here these two days [wrote Horace Walpole from Stowe in 1753], extremely amused and charmed indeed. Wherever you stand you see an Albano landscape. Half as many buildings I believe would be too many, but such a profusion gives inexpressible richness . . . But I have no patience at building and planting a satire! Such is the temple of modern virtue in ruins! [The Earl had erected a ruin, which he called the Temple of Modern Virtue.] The Grecian temple is glorious: this I openly worship: in the heretical corner of my heart I adore the Gothick building, which by some unusual inspiration Gibbs has made pure and beautiful and venerable. The style has a propensity to the Venetian or mosque Gothick, and the great column near it makes the whole put one in mind of the Place of St. Mark.

The Albano landscape which Walpole saw had been planned by Bridgeman, under the general inspiration of Vanbrugh; but it was never realized according to the Bridgeman plan. It grew from that start, changing with the whims of successive owners and architects, until, by the end of the century, after the work of Capability Brown, it had reached something like its present proportions. When Walpole first visited Stowe — which incidentally seems to have been pronounced in his day to rhyme with 'plough' — he would not have found the Corinthian Arch which now graces the Buckingham avenue, nor the avenue itself. Much of the woodland which began round the Ridings would not yet have crept south; the trees themselves would have been young; and perhaps several of the present temples would have been to come. It is impossible to be sure what he found.

In visiting the completed glory which now exists as a public school, however, he would have entered the gates at the edge of the town, and would have driven for miles[1] along an avenue of elms and beeches — straight as a Roman road — over undulating country. The last undulation would have brought him within sight of an arc-de-triomphe, like the one at Marble Arch but less fussy, standing golden and assimilated in the afternoon sun. Having mounted the avenue to this edifice, he would have been met by a beadle in livery, under whose directions the gate of the arch would have been opened, and a brazen bell, like a small church bell, would have been rung to warn the house-servants, still a mile away. The Corinthian Arch was a dwelling-house for the beadle and for his underlings, being pierced with windows and doors on the sides not visible from the avenue. Framed in the huge aperture, while the gates were being dragged apart, he would have caught his first

---

[1] The total distance from Stowe to Buckingham was given by the surveyors in 1744 as 7 miles, 2 roods, 135 yards.

THE SCANDALMONGER

glimpse of the palace itself: far across lakes and green lawns, aureate, like the arch, with the warm ochre of its south front, faintly resembling Buckingham Palace, but wider and more Doric and slumbering on the ridge of a gentle rise in the green vista of forest.

If he had paused there, to examine the wonderful scene, he might have been able, before the trees grew to their twentieth-century magnificence, to see the Palladian Bridge on his right, over the uppermost of the lakes; perhaps a trace of the Temple of Friendship; the two small temples beside the middle lake, with a few grottos and a monument to Congreve; the Temple of Venus beside the next lake; the Oxford Bridge below the last of them, and the Boycott Pavilions through which his avenue would eventually lead him. The lowest stretch of water has since been called the Copper Bottom — because one of the Dukes was believed to have copper-plated it, to see if it would look better. In all, the lakes covered about twenty acres. It was Walpole himself who nicely dubbed the view they footed 'that Province which they call a garden'.

The arch only gave the pre-view, however. The family name of the Dukes of Buckingham had been Temple (it ended as something like Plantaganet Campbell Temple Nugent Brydges Chandos Grenville), and this seems to have had an effect upon their interests. Taking the whole Province, and counting obelisks, columns, arches, grottos, monopteroi, etc., there were some twenty temples in the grounds — the largest big enough for Paestum, the smallest a mere pyramid with a monkey on it, not too big for a mausoleum. It must have been like owning a private

A PRIVATE PAESTUM

Paestum in the Palladian style; though why anybody should wish to own a Paestum, or what he would do with it if he did, apart from having picnics in the temples, was a matter for the Dukes themselves. They could have had tea in a different monument every day for three weeks. 'As far as the mere pleasure of seeing goes,' wrote the younger Pitt in 1783, in some perplexity, 'I had rather be the visitor than the owner.'

So stupendous does the pleasure of seeing remain, however, that it is difficult to choose a starting point for a description. Perhaps it should be with the trees; though we see them now in greater beauty than they could have offered to Walpole. For all the temples, and the long yet fitting palace of gold, were set down in a forest which was not a jungle, in a tamed Arcadian woodland whose undergrowth had been controlled and whose disposition had been managed, without being regimented. Except for the formal avenues, there were no straight lines. The walks and valleys strolled gently from one view to another, ready to lead the enchanted wanderer from a Gothick temple after his own heart to a column like Nelson's in Trafalgar Square, or from a shell grotto to a little waterfall. The leaves were round about, shutting out until they were ready to reveal, tempting the foot tactfully to visit one more Albano. They represented not only the common trees, in thousands, but also charming imports: sequoias, tulip trees, cedars, acacia, black walnut.

The pleasure-ground extended to about a thousand acres, in which and from which no trace of tillage could be seen. The only farmhouse visible from the furthest spinney had been built to look like a castle, to the permanent discomfort of its tenant. There were two other avenues, apart from the Buckingham one, by which the whole could be approached. When the Dukes had finally ruined themselves, it was said that they owned leases all the fifty or sixty miles from Stowe to London, because they 'liked to drive on their own land'.

After leaving the Triumphal Arch, the Buckingham avenue swerved through the deer-park to the west, joined the Oxford avenue at the Boycott Pavilions, and made its way to the north front. Here there was an equestrian statue of George II, and the colonnades made the façade look a little like St. Peter's at Rome, although on a smaller scale and without the dome.

On both fronts there were flights of steps to mount, more numerous than those at the British Museum. There were fountains, hot-houses, a menagerie, a museum, stables for countless horses. In the priceless library, there were the rarest editions, manuscripts including the *Annals of the Four Masters*, and a supposed portrait of Shakespeare. There was also the timid librarian, Charles O'Connor, who believed that he was being starved to death. He was known as 'the Abbé', and walked to Buckingham every day with his gold-headed cane, reading a book. In the state dining-room, with its two Grinling Gibbons overmantels, there was a dining-table exactly as long as a cricket pitch.

'Henry', wrote Sir Andrew Barnard in 1821, 'was delighted with his short visit at Stowe . . . Ly Buckingham . . . asked Henry to a domestic party as they are quite alone — they sat to dinner 95.'

The Duchess of Buckingham told me that, when

A PRIVATE PAESTUM

George the Fourth slept at Stowe in the statebed-chamber (which has a good deal of ebony furniture), it was lighted up with a vast number of wax candles, which were kept burning the whole night. Nobody, I imagine, except a king, has any liking for a state bed-chamber. I was at Cassiobury with a large party, when a gentleman arrived, to whom Lord Essex said, 'I must put you into the state bedroom, as it is the only one unoccupied.' The gentleman, rather than sleep in it, took up his quarters at the inn.

SAMUEL ROGERS

It was to this astonishing Olympus that Horace was summoned again in 1770, to amuse the Princess Amelia, who was on a visit. It was in the framework of these colossal columns, and down these avalanches of stone steps, that their anticlimax of a retinue hobbled and stumbled to its evening entertainment — a gouty harlequinade of Rowlandson figures, against the grandeur and serenity of Pugin.

The party passed off [he wrote on July 7th] much better than I expected. A Princess at the head of a very small set for five days together did not promise well. However, she was very good-humoured, and easy, and dispensed with a large quantity of etiquette. Lady Temple is good-nature itself, my lord was very civil, Lord Besborough is made to suit all sorts of people, Lady Mary Coke respects royalty too much not to be very condescending, Lady Anne Howard and Mrs. Middleton filled up the drawing-room, or rather made it out, and I was so determined to carry it off as well as I could, and happened to be in such good spirits, and took such care to avoid politics, that we laughed a great deal, and had not a cloud the whole time.
We breakfasted at half an hour after nine; but the Princess did not appear till it was finished; then we

walked in the garden, or drove about in cabriolets, till it was time to dress; dined at three, which, though properly proportioned to the smallness of the company to avoid ostentation, lasted a vast while, as the Princess eats and talks a great deal; then again into the garden till past seven, when we came in, drank tea and coffee, and played at pharaoh till ten, when the Princess retired, and we went to supper, and before twelve to bed. You see there was great sameness and little vivacity in all this. It was a little broken by fishing, and going round the park one of the mornings; but in reality the number of buildings and variety of scenes in the garden made each day different from the rest: and my meditations on so historic a spot prevented my being tired. Every acre brings to one's mind some instance of parts or pedantry, of the taste or want of taste, of the ambition, or love of fame, or greatness, or miscarriages of those that have inhabited, decorated, planned, or visited the place. Pope, Congreve, Vanbrugh, Kent, Gibbs, Lord Cobham, Lord Chesterfield, the mob of nephews, the Lytteltons, Grenvilles, Wests, Leonidas Glover and Wilkes, the late Prince of Wales, the King of Denmark, Princess Amelie, and the proud monuments of Lord Chatham's services, now enshrined there, then anathematised there, and now again commanding there, with the Temple of Friendship like the Temple of Janus, sometimes open to war, and sometimes shut up in factious cabals, all these images crowd upon one's memory and add visionary personages to the charming scenes, that are so enriched with fanes and temples, that the real prospects are little less than visions themselves.

On Wednesday night a small Vauxhall was acted for us at the grotto in the Elysian fields, which was illuminated with lamps, as were the thicket and two little barks on the lake. With a little exaggeration I could make you believe that nothing ever was so delightful. The idea was really pretty, but as my feelings

A PRIVATE PAESTUM

have lost some of their romantic sensibility, I did not quite enjoy such an entertainment *al fresco* so much as I should have done twenty years ago. The evening was more than cool, and the destined spot anything but dry. There were not half lamps enough, and no music but an ancient militia-man who played cruelly on a squeaking tabor and pipe. As our procession descended the vast flight of steps into the garden, in which was assembled a crowd of people from Buckingham and the neighbouring villages to see the Princess and the show, the moon shining very bright, I could not help laughing, as I surveyed our troop, which instead of tripping lightly to such an Arcadian entertainment, were hobbling down, by the balustrades, wrapped up in cloaks and great-coats for fear of catching cold. The Earl you know is bent double, the Countess very lame, I am a miserable walker, and the Princess, though as strong as a Brunswic lion, makes no figure in going down fifty stone stairs. Except Lady Ann — and by courtesy, Lady Mary, we were none of us young enough for a pastoral. We supped in the grotto, which is as proper to this climate, as a sea-coal fire would be in the dog-days at Tivoli.

But the chief entertainment of the week, at least what was so to the Princess, is an arch which Lord Temple has erected to her honour in the most enchanting of all picturesque scenes. It is inscribed on one side *Ameliae Sophiae Aug.* and has a medallion of her on the other. It is placed on an eminence at the top of the Elysian fields, in a grove of orange trees. You come to it on a sudden, and are startled with delight on looking through it: you at once see through a glade the river winding at bottom; from which a thicket rises, arched over with trees, but opened, and discovering a hillock full of hay-cocks, beyond which in front is the Palladian bridge, and again over that, a larger hill crowned with the castle. It is a tall landscape, framed by the arch and the overbowering trees, and comprehending more beauties of light, shade, and buildings, than any picture of Albano I ever saw. Between the flattery and the prospect the Princess was really in Elysium: she visited her arch four and five times every day, and could not satiate herself with it. The statues of Apollo and the Muses stand on each side of the arch. One day she found in Apollo's hand the following lines, which I had written for her and communicated to Lord Temple,

> T'other day with a beautiful frown on her brow
> To the rest of the gods said the Venus of Stowe,
> 'What a fuss is here made with that arch just erected!
> How *our* temples are slighted, our altars neglected!
> Since yon nymph has appear'd, *we* are noticed no more:
> All resort to *her* shrine, all *her* presence adore.
> And what's more provoking, before all our faces
> Temple thither has drawn both the Muses and Graces.'
> 'Keep your temper, dear child,' Phoebus cried with a smile,
> 'Nor this happy, this amiable festival spoil.
> Can your shrine any longer with garlands be drest?—
> When a true goddess reigns, all the false are supprest.'

If you will keep my counsel, I will own to you, that originally the two last lines were much better, but I was forced to alter them out of decorum, not to be too pagan upon the occasion; in short, here they are as in the first sketch,

> 'Recollect, once before that our oracles ceas'd,
> When a real divinity rose in the East.'

So many heathen temples around, had made me talk as a Roman poet would have done: but I corrected my verses, and have made them insipid enough to offend nobody. Good night! I am rejoiced to be once more in the gay solitude of my own little Tempe.

A PRIVATE PAESTUM

He wrote about it again to Conway on the 12th, from his own Tempe, playing with his ideas and improving on them, as he always did:

Reposing under my laurels! No, no, I am reposing in a much better tent, under the tester of my own bed. I am not obliged to rise by break of day and be dressed for the drawing-room; I may saunter in my slippers till dinner-time, and not make bows till my back is as much out of joint as my Lord Temple's. In short, I should die of the gout or fatigue, if I was to be Polonius to a Princess for another week. Twice a-day we made a pilgrimage to almost every heathen temple in that Province which they call a garden; and there is no sallying out of the house without descending a flight of steps as high as St. Paul's. My Lord Besborough would have dragged me up to the top of the column, to see all the kingdoms of the earth; but I would not, if he could have given them to me. To crown all, because we live under the line, and that we were all of us giddy young creatures, of near threescore, we supped in a grotto in the Elysian fields, and were refreshed with rivers of dew and gentle showers that dripped from all the trees, and put us in mind of the heroic ages, when kings and queens were shepherds and shepherdesses, and lived in caves, and were wet to the skin two or three times a day. Well! thank Heaven, I am emerged from that Elysium, and once more in a Christian country!— Not but, to say the truth, our pagan landlord and landlady were very obliging, and the party went off much better than I expected.

When he was an old man getting on for seventy, thinking back to the many great houses which he had seen, 'Stowe', he wrote, 'I know by heart . . . and the vastness pleases me more than I can defend'. It was a sincere compliment, for he had never been a slave to mere size. He had described the heavy load of Blenheim as being like 'the palace of an auctioneer, who has been chosen King of Poland'. It was architecturally, not financially, that he had been overwhelmed by the 'inexpressible richness'.

The Dukes were 'enemies of the People', it is true, who 'ground the faces of the poor'. Fortunately for those days, however, the nasty and needless hatred between abstract economic levels had yet to be invented. People lived well, even the country poor. 'Beef and mutton', says Lecky, 'were eaten almost daily in villages where their use had before been hardly known . . . Wheat bread, and that of the finest flour.' 'In England', wrote Arthur Young on one of his tours, 'the quantity of meat, butter and cheese consumed by all ranks of the people was immense.'

Under the first two Georges [says G. M. Trevelyan] the wage-earner, both in town and country, scarcely seems to have resented at all his want of social and political power . . . And even if he had no vote, he could stand cheering or hooting in front of the hustings, while the candidate, possibly a Peer's son, bowed low with his hand on his heart and a rotten egg in his hair, addressing the mob as 'gentlemen' and asking for their support as the chief object of his ambition. The sight filled foreign visitors with admiration and astonishment. The spirit of aristocracy and the spirit of popular rights seemed to have arrived at a perfect harmony, peculiar to the England of that epoch. There have been worse relations than that between rich and poor, between governors and governed. There was no class hatred, and though highest and lowest were far apart, there were infinite gradations and no rigid class barriers as on the Continent.

The inhabitants of Dadford and of Buckingham,

who went to view the junketing at the Great House, and to help the mirth along with pipe and tabor, were proud that their own Duke should be patronized by a royal princess, because it conferred a secondary greatness on themselves.

'Yes, sure, ma'am,' [an old baker-woman told Fanny Burney, after a royal visit to Sidmouth], 'we all did our best then, for there was ne'er a town in all England like Sidmouth for rejoicing. Why, I baked a hundred and ten penny loaves for the poor, and so did every baker in the town, and there's three; and the gentry subscribed for it. And the gentry roasted a bullock and cut it all up, and we all eat it, in the midst of the rejoicing. And then we had such a fine sermon, it made us all cry; there was a more tears shed than ever was known, all for over-joy. And they had the King drawed, and dressed up all in gold and laurels, and they put un in a coach and eight horses, and carried un about; and all the grand gentlemen in the town, and all abouts, came in their own carriages to join. And they had the finest band in all England singing "God save the King," and every soul joined in the chorus, and all not so much because he was a king, but because they said a was such a worthy gentleman, and that the like of him was never known in this nation before; so we all subscribed for the illuminations for that reason, — some a shilling, some a guinea, some a penny, — for no one begrudged it, as a was such a worthy person.'

At Stowe they were equally proud of worth, when the great Earl of Chatham came on a visit 'in a jim-whiskee drawn by two horses', with a train of 'two coaches and six, with twenty servants male and female'. They were prouder when the exiled King of France went to live there, or when Queen Victoria held the only Drawing-room ever held before outside a royal palace. If the villagers approved of their own Duke, they liked him to be grand. He was their Lord Mayor's Show, who stirred them with a spectacle. They too were vain of vast possessions, and of the land he owned from thence to London. If, on the other hand, they disapproved, the London chairmen formed a mob, and smashed his windows.

Incidentally, when the lower classes were brought into contact with the aristocracy, as domestic servants in these palaces, their treatment was personal, and better than it was to become under Victoria. Swift had been accustomed to beat his Irish valet, and the ungovernable Mr. Lambton, the first Earl of Durham, was to try to do so again in 1824.

The night before last [wrote Creevey] between 12 and 1, I being in the library where the same cold fowl always is with wine and water, Lambton came in out of the hazard room, and, finding no water, begun belabouring the bell in a way that I thought must inevitably have brought the whole concern down. No effect was produced, so he sallied forth, evidently boiling, and when he returned he said: 'I don't think I shall have to ring so long another time.' This is all I know of my own knowledge but, says Lady Augusta Milbanke to me yesterday — 'Do you know what happened last night?' — 'Du tout,' says I. — 'Why,' says she, 'Mr. Lambton rung the bell for water so long, that he went and rung the house bell, when his own man came; and upon saying something in his own justification which displeased the Monarch, he laid hold of a stick and struck him twice; upon which his man told him he could not stand that, and that if he did it again he should be obliged to knock him down. So the master held his hand and the man gave him notice he had done with him.'

A PRIVATE PAESTUM

Between Lambton and Swift, however, before Victoria and after Anne, the masters seem to have behaved admirably, and to have been adopted as a species of paterfamilias by their menials. At Chatsworth, says Farington, the Duke 'kills on an average 5 bullocks in a fortnight and 15 or 16 sheep a week . . . The Duke is a very quiet man, who gives no trouble to any one'. Miss Burney's relations with her footman Colomb were touching. The housekeeper of Daniel Day, the rich pump and block maker, 'had two very strong attachments, one to her wedding-ring and garments, and the other to tea; when she died, Mr. Day would not permit her ring to be taken off, he said, "If that was attempted, she would come to life again," and directed that she should be buried in her wedding suit and a pound of tea in each hand; and these directions were literally obeyed'.

Hogarth painted all his servants on one canvas. Dr. Johnson's maidservant, Catherine Chambers, lived with the family from sixteen to fifty-eight, when she died. On her death-bed, he recorded, 'She told me that to part was the greatest pain she had ever felt, and that she hoped we should meet again in a better place. I expressed, with swelled eyes and great emotion of tenderness, the same hopes. We kissed and parted.' Lady Mary Bertie always felt like getting up to curtsy when her maid came into the room — and no wonder, for that maid ended up as Mrs. Siddons. Later, at the height of her fame, Mrs. Siddons revisited her employer's house and was honourably received, without shyness on either side. Princess Amelia's maid, Mary Gaskoin, is buried near her mistress in St. George's Chapel, Windsor.

THE SCANDALMONGER

Horace Walpole's domestics were treated as well as his dogs, which was as well as they could be treated. Men lived and died in his employment, and it was left to him to bury them. In fact, he was unable to get rid of servants, even when he desired it.

I have a gardener that has lived with me above five-and-twenty years; he is incredibly ignorant, and a mule. When I wrote to your Lordship, my patience was worn out, and I resolved at least to have a gardener for flowers. On your not being able to give me one, I half consented to keep my own; not on his amendment, but because he will not leave me, presuming on my long suffering. I have offered him fifteen pounds a year to leave me, and when he pleads that he is old, and that nobody else will take him, I plead that I am old too, and that it is rather hard that I am not to have a few flowers, or a little fruit as long as I live.

The high-water mark of tyranny was reached by the domestics of Hannah More, who ended by driving her out of house and home.

The occasion of quitting my darling abode at Barley Wood was occasioned by a sudden and accidental discovery of the atrocities which were carrying on in my family [household] every night after I was in bed. I grieve for the honour of human nature to say that the ringleader had lived with me 26 years; the Coachman 18 and so on. At ten o'clock as soon as I was in bed, and I thought they were so too, their Party from the village arrived and they all sat down to the nightly festivity, consisting of game (if it was to be had at any price), or a Turkey, or ducks. Tea with the finest pastry covered a large table, my silver forks, Candlesticks etc., rum brandy or gin followed during the greatest part of the night; they not only went to bed shockingly intoxicated, but I have known them go to bed before dinner with a second drunkenness, palmed on me for a bad head ache. When the festivity was to be particularly grand, and a band of music attended, the supper was celebrated in my Coachhouse, my doors of course left open — and poor I asleep. As I had not been downstairs for years, I knew nothing that passed there. My friends thought all was not right, but kindly tho' imprudently kept it from me: I found my expenses immense: but was imposed upon by false tradesmen's Bills. I immediately resolved to quit the place. To turn them away would have been useless, as they had built and planted little spots of their own. . . .

The majority of domestic stories were not so tragic as this. It was typical of the period that a household should have been known as a 'family'. No servant ever left the employment of Sydney Smith, except to be married or to be buried, and his relations with his eccentric staff form a pleasant contrast to those of the Earl of Durham.

'Come here, Bunch!' (calling out to her), 'come and repeat your crimes to Mrs. Marcet'; and Bunch, a clean, fair, squat, tidy little girl, about ten or twelve years of age, quite as a matter of course, as grave as a judge, without the least hesitation, and with a loud voice, began to repeat — 'Plate-snatching, gravy-spilling, door-slamming, blue-bottle fly-catching, and curtsy-bobbing.' 'Explain to Mrs. Marcet what blue-bottle fly-catching is.' 'Standing with my mouth open and not attending, Sir.' 'And what is curtsy-bobbing?' 'Curtsying to the centre of the earth, please, Sir.' 'Good girl; now you may go. She makes a capital waiter, I assure you; on *state* occasions Jack Robinson, my carpenter, takes off his apron and waits too, and does pretty well, but he sometimes naturally makes a mistake and sticks a gimlet into the bread instead of a fork.'

THE SCANDALMONGER

At Stowe, where there were 400 gardeners employed, the staff formed a hierarchy as definite as that above stairs. From the housekeeper and the upper servants like the butler, to the least of the gardeners' boys, the domestics stood in their own ranks, knowing who stood above and below.

The glorious house and province seems always to have exercised a soothing effect upon its visitors. In 1747, two learned deists went there 'to examine critically the scriptures at their leisure, and put together all the contradictions and impossibilities they fancied they should find in order to hurt Christianity the more, but behold,' wrote the Earl of Egmont in high delight, 'the result was that the two men I speak of returned convinced of errors and resolved to do their best to undeceive others.'

It was a patriarchal society, and, though the splendours of the Duke may have been palatial, the comforts of his employees were benevolently considered. The socialist agitator of the twentieth century, so constantly bawling about the 'starvation wages' of his ancestors, always overlooks through malevolence or ignorance the fact that the pound sterling itself has utterly altered in value. He will have noted with indignation that Horace Walpole only offered his gardener £15 a year as a bribe to leave his service. Before we agree with socialist lamentations, however, it would be worth finding out what fifteen pounds was really worth.

In 1763, during the hey-day of the Age of Scandal, Jamie Boswell applied to Dr. Johnson for advice about the cost of living. The amiable doctor knew all about it, from his own bitter experience of earlier years in

A PRIVATE PAESTUM

Grub Street, and money was a matter of moment to Boswell himself, owing to the continuous clash between his generous nature and his native respect for the bawbee. It was the great man's opinion that one could sustain life on £6 a year, or live in reasonable comfort on £30 a year.

Sir [said he], if you want merely to support nature, Sir William Petty fixes your allowance at three pounds a year. But as times are much altered, we shall call it six. This will fill your belly, shelter you from the weather, and even get you a strong lasting coat, supposing it made of good bull's hide. Now, Sir, all beyond this is artificial taste, and is desired in order to obtain a greater degree of respect from our fellow-creatures.

Of the higher level in comfort the doctor gave the following estimate.

At my last meeting with Mr. Johnson, he said that when he came first to London and was upon his shifts, he was told by a very clever man who understood perfectly the common affairs of life that £30 a year was enough to make a man live without being contemptible; that is to say, you might be always clean. He allowed £10 for clothes and linen. He said you might live in a garret at eighteen-pence a week, as few people would inquire where you lodge; and, if they do, it is easy to say, 'Sir, I am to be found at such a place.' [i.e. Do not give your address, but agree to meet at a coffee house.] For spending threepence in a coffee-house, you may be for hours in very good company. You may dine for sixpence, you may breakfast on bread and milk, and you may want supper.

So much for the modest demands of a man-of-letters. Boswell, however, was a young man about

THE SCANDALMONGER

town. He had hob-nobbed with the Duke of York, and still did hob-nob with such distinguished people as the Duchess of Northumberland or the Duke of Queensberry or the Earl of Eglinton. He was a candidate for a commission in the Guards. In his own scheme of living, he felt that 'a genteel lodging in a good part of the town is absolutely necessary'. (He got one in Downing Street, 'with the use of a handsome parlour all the forenoon'.) He also felt it necessary that he should have a fire in his dining-room, wax candles, clean linen every day, a hair-dresser to call on him daily, and 'I must have my shoes wiped at least once a day and sometimes oftener'. In 1762 he sat down cannily to add up a budget for this kind of life — though unfortunately, by confusing Washing with Hairdressing, he added it up wrong.

Lodging	£50
Dinner	18
Breakfast	9
Candles	6
Coals	7
Washing	6
Shoe-cleaning	1
Clothes	50
Stockings & shoes	10

In all, £157

Even if he had remembered to enter the Hairdressing, the yearly budget of this young aristocrat who was sowing his wild oats, entertaining and living in Downing Street, would only have amounted to a necessary sum of £164.

There, then, are three standards of eighteenth-century living, none of them falling below the standard of

A PRIVATE PAESTUM

sufficient food, clothing and shelter: £6 a year for the poor clerk, £30 a year for the author and £164 a year for the young Guardee.

In fact, leaving all thoughts of modern income taxes aside — and private enterprise in the eighteenth century was not crippled by income tax — the pound of those days was worth much more than ten of ours. Horace Walpole was offering his gardener more than twice Dr. Johnson's estimate of a living wage — merely to go away.

It is true that at the top of the social tree there were palaces like Stowe and noblemen like the Earl of Durham, who felt that it was possible 'to jog along on £40,000 a year', but the sufferings at the foot of the tree have been exaggerated by politicians.

Frederic Eden [we learn from Mr. Arthur Bryant, in his *Age of Elegance*], in his survey of the condition of the poor made during the famine years of 1795 and 1796, analysed the budget of a Leicester woolcomber with two children, who, out of an income of £47 a year, made up of his own and his wife's and his elder son's earnings and an £11 grant from the Poor Law guardians, was able to buy weekly ten pounds of butcher's meat, two pounds of butter, three and a half of cheese and about nineteen pints of milk, as well as potatoes, vegetables, tea, sugar and beer. He was not even a particularly industrious man, for he was said to spend several days every month in an alehouse lamenting the hardness of the times. Another case instanced by Eden was that of a Manchester dyer who only earned, with his wife's help, £42 p.a., yet bought five pounds of meat weekly. Even in the work-houses meat usually figured on the dietary three or four days a week. When six Lancashire weavers were consigned by the Home Office to the Cold Bath Fields prison on a charge of treason, they were allowed between them for breakfast six pound-loaves of bread, two pounds of butter, two of sugar and one of tea, for dinner a quarter of pork with vegetables, potatoes and a pot of porter apiece, and for supper cold meat and tea. On another day they were given a leg of mutton weighing thirteen and a half pounds.

That Leicestershire woolcomber in 1795 — who was receiving public assistance — could afford for his family ten pounds of meat every week. Had he lived in the English Socialist Paradise of 1951, when the Dukes have been expelled from Stowe and their lovely Elysium turned into a Public School, he would have been rationed to 16 ounces of steak per week between the four of them.

CHAPTER TEN

Fire! Fire!

DEAR Mason [wrote the poet Gray in 1759], I am extremely obliged to you for the kind attention you bestow on me and my affairs. I have not been a sufferer by this calamity; it was on the other side of the street, and did not reach so far as the houses opposite to mine; but there was an attorney who had writings belonging to me in his hands, that had his house burnt down among the first, yet he has had the good fortune to save all his papers. The fire is said to have begun in the chamber of that poor glass-organist who lodged at a coffee-house in Swithin's Alley, and perished in the flames. Two other persons were destroyed (in the charitable office of assisting their friends) by the fall of some buildings. Last night there was another fire in Lincoln's Inn Fields, that burnt the Sardinian Ambassador's chapel and stables, with some adjacent houses. 'Tis strange that we all of us (here in town) lay ourselves down every night on our funeral pile, ready made, and compose ourselves to rest, while every drunken footman and drowsy old woman has a candle ready to light it before morning.

It was an age of calamities, of alarms and excursions — the kind of age which was to colour the pages of Hilaire Belloc, in which little boys expired from eating string or little girls were burnt to death for telling fibs. Many of the alarms took place by fire, and Gray himself had lost a house, in Cornhill, in 1748.

I quit politics [wrote Horace Walpole in 1763] to tell

THE SCANDALMONGER

you the most melancholy catastrophe, that one almost ever heard or read of. The house of Lady Molesworth, in Upper Brook Street, was suddenly burnt to the ground last Friday, between four and five in the morning. Herself, two of her daughters, her brother, and three servants perished, with all the circumstances of horror imaginable! The house, which was small, happened to be crowded, by the arrival of her brother, Captain Usher, from Jamaica, who lay there but that night for the first time, and by a visit from Dr. Molesworth (her brother-in-law) and his wife. The doctor waked, hearing what he thought hail. He rose, opened the window and saw nothing. The noise increased, he opened the door, and found the whole staircase in flames and smoke. Seeing no retreat, he would have persuaded his wife to rush with him into the smoke, and perish at once, as the quickest death. She had not resolution enough. He then flung out a mattress for her to jump on (it was two pair of stairs backwards): while he was doing this he saw from the garret above one of the young ladies leap into the back court. Mrs. Molesworth then jumped out of the window, and was scarce hurt; he clambered out too, and hung by a hook: a man from the back of another house saw him, and called to him that he would bring a ladder; he did, but it was too short. However, he begged the doctor, if possible, to hang there still, which, though his strength, for he is a very old man, almost failed him, he did and was saved; but he is since grown so disordered with the terror and calamity, that they doubt if he will live. Lady Molesworth, who lay two pairs of stairs forewards, and who, to make room, had taken her eldest daughter, of seventeen, to lie with her, was seen by persons in the street at the window: the daughter jumped into the street, fell on the iron spikes, and thence into the area. Lady Molesworth was at the other window in her shift, and lifted up her hands, either to open the sash, or in agonies for

FIRE! FIRE!

her daughter, but suddenly disappeared. Some think that the floor at that instant fell with her; I rather conclude that she swooned when her daughter leaped, and never recovered.
The young lady has had her leg cut off, and has not been in her senses since. The youngest daughter, about nine or ten, had the quickness to get out at window on the top of the house, but from spikes and chimneys could get no further. She went back to her room where her governess was, who jumped first, and was dashed to pieces. The child then jumped, and was little hurt, though burnt, and almost stifled by the bedclothes which Dr. Molesworth flung out, for this was her that he saw. They told her that her governess was safe; she replied, 'Don't pretend to make me believe that, for I saw her dead on the pavement, and her brains scattered about.'
Another of the sisters jumped too, and escaped with a fractured thigh. A footman, who lay below, and could have saved himself easily, ran up to try to save some of the family, but being involved in flames and much burnt, was forced to try the window, fell on the spikes like Miss Molesworth, but they think will live. Lord Molesworth, the only son, a boy at Westminster, was at home that day, and was to have lain there, but not having done his task, was obliged to go back to school, and was thus fortunately preserved.

Now Gray was one of the many bachelors of the period, like his friend Horry Walpole or like George Selwyn, and, although he was a charming letter-writer, he was inclined to be fussy. He was the only child that had survived infancy, from a family of twelve. His constitution was a feeble one; he had an affected pronunciation, and would say 'What naise [noise] is that?'; he passed the greater part of his life in college at Cambridge, where he formed a stiff, romantic attachment to two young undergraduates; he was so shy in society that the only thing he said, when spending a day with Lady Ailesbury, was 'Yes, my lady, I believe so'; he lived in solitude and seclusion to such an extent that, when he did leave his hibernaculum, 'he was accompanied by Dr. Gisborne, Mr. Stonhewer, and Mr. Palgrave, and they walked one after one, in Indian file' while, 'when they withdrew, every college man took off his cap as he passed, a considerable number having assembled in the quadrangle to see Mr. Gray, who was seldom seen'; during the chief part of his life he 'kept a *daily* record of the blowing of flowers, the leafing of trees, the state of the thermometer, the quarter from which the wind blew, and the falling of rain', entering these, in his minute, melancholic handwriting, 'with the utmost precision, and sometimes into a naturalist's calendar in addition'; he also kept a daily record in Latin of his health; his marginalia to works of every kind gave one critic the impression that he was the 'most learned man in Europe'; and 'to him, the Genealogical Researches of Dugdale were incomplete; the scientific language of Linnaeus imperfect; and the History of the Chinese Dynasties, in fifteen quarto volumes, by Grosier, needed his verbal corrections, and supplemental improvements, before it was worthy of being enrolled in the archives of Pekin'.

Unfortunately, however, Gray suffered from a trifling weakness. He was afraid of fire. What was still more unfortunate, the undergraduates of an ancient university seem always to have enjoyed their little joke.

Mr. Gray set himself to cope with the incendiary

problem as well as he could. He scanned the faces of any friends who happened to have been burnt out, discovering in one of them 'evident marks of terror', two or three days after the disaster. He insured himself with the London Assurance Office in Birchen Lane. He purchased from a reliable firm in the metropolis a stout rope-ladder, and sat down at last with stoic calm, in 1756, in his rooms at Peterhouse, to await the event.

The undergraduates considered it a shame that so much preparation should be made in vain. They put a tub under the poet's window after nightfall, and sounded the alarm.

Mr. Gray's drill was perfect. He did not wait to try the door. He threw open the window in his nightcap, ejected the rope-ladder, and clambered over the sill. The immortal author of the *Elegy in a Country Churchyard* lowered himself carefully to the end of the rope and placed himself, with deadly accuracy, in the middle of the butt of water.

CHAPTER ELEVEN

Bribery and Corruption

A SINGULAR transition which started during the second half of the eighteenth century was that which led from the political corruption of Walpole's 'placemen' to the almost morbid sense of responsibility visible in the Victorian parliaments of Greville.

In the early days of the Age of Reason, election to parliament had been mainly by money and violence, by clubs, brandy bottles and gold. The *Flying Post* of January 27th, 1715, printed the following imaginary 'Bill of Costs' for an election:

	£	s.	d.
Imprimis, for bespeaking and collecting a mob	20	0	0
Item, for many suits of knots for their heads	30	0	0
For scores of huzza-men	40	0	0
For roarers of the word 'Church'	40	0	0
For a set of 'No Roundhead' roarers	40	0	0
For several gallons of Tory punch on church tombstones	30	0	0
For a majority of clubs and brandy bottles	20	0	0
For bell-ringers, fiddlers and porters	10	0	0
For a set of coffee-house praters	40	0	0
For extraordinary expense for cloth's and lac'd hats on show days, to dazzle the mob	50	0	0
For Dissenters' damners	40	0	0
For demolishing two houses	200	0	0

BRIBERY AND CORRUPTION

	£	s.	d.
For committing two riots	200	0	0
For secret encouragement to the rioters	40	0	0
For a dozen of perjury men	100	0	0
For packing and carriage paid to Gloucester	50	0	0
For breaking windows	20	0	0
For a gang of alderman-abusers	40	0	0
For a set of notorious lyars	50	0	0
For pot-ale	100	0	0
For law, and charges in the King's Bench	300	0	0
	£1460	0	0

In Ireland, where anachronisms always persist for a century or two, the custom of election by violence continued to the reign of George IV, if not far beyond. The latter monarch said to an Irish candidate: 'I hear you are to have an election in Galway: who will win?' He was told: 'The survivor, sire.'

In England, as the Age of Reason began to merge into the Age of Scandal, the simple payment of five guineas to each voter for his support in a cheap borough, began to replace the expenditure on armaments. The new system, though more humane and easier to work, was more expensive. As against the £1460 of 1715, we find Wilberforce paying some £8500 for his seat. In 1790, it cost Castlereagh £60,000 to get in for the County Down, while the 'Austerlitz of Electioneering', which was fought in 1807, is said to have mulcted the three candidates for Yorkshire to the tune of half a million.

THE SCANDALMONGER

Once in, there were still expenses to be met:

R. B. SHERIDAN, ESQ., EXPENSES AT THE BOROUGH OF STAFFORD, FOR ELECTION, ANNO 1784

	£	s.	d.
248 Burgesses paid £5 5s. each	1302	0	0

YEARLY EXPENSES SINCE

	£	s.	d.			
House rent and taxes	23	6	6			
Servant at 6s. per week, Board Wages	15	12	0			
Ditto, yearly wages	8	8	0			
Coals &c.	10	0	0			
				57	6	6
Ale tickets	40	0	0			
Half the Members' Plate	25	0	0			
Swearing young Burgesses	10	0	0			
Subscriptions to the Infirmary	5	5	0			
Do., Clergymen's Widows	2	2	0			
Ringers	4	4	0			
				86	11	0
One year				143	17	6
Multiplied by years				× 6		
				863	5	0

Total expense of six years' parliament, exclusive of expenses incurred during the time of election and your own annual expenses .. £2165 5 0

MOORE's *Life of Sheridan*

CHAIRING THE MEMBER

BRIBERY AND CORRUPTION

The payment of five guineas to each voter only obtained at the cheaper seats. In Ilchester, the vote of a 'plumper' cost as much as £40.

As late as 1820, it was calculated that 353 members of parliament were nominated by only 187 Englishmen. Many of the boroughs were rotten; some were represented by only one voter who might return two members; the stability of any ministry depended upon the count of its supporters in the House. Consequently, since the sinecures and rich 'places' were in the gift of the ministry, these presents were awarded to borough-owners who could offer a *quid pro quo* by returning gentlemen who would vote for the ministry. The minister gave a sinecure to the landlord or to the member for his allegiance, the member gave a bribe to the voter for his, the sinecure in the last resort being salaried from the taxes paid by the voter: a vicious circle. Other corruptions were common. Apart from jerry-mandering about the 'counts', free liquor and hired mobs of bruisers, sailors or Irish chair-men to break up the poll, there was always the chance that the King might send the Household troops to vote, or that the landlord might evict opponents, or that the drivers of conveyances bringing supporters to the booths might be bribed to take them elsewhere. Voters who were being conveyed by water, all coaches having been 'bought up', sometimes awoke with a hangover to find themselves in Norway or Holland.

Such was the state of affairs at the acme of the Age of Scandal, a position which had led Sir Robert Walpole to declare that every man had his price, and which led his son Horace to retire from parliament, only too glad to wash his hands of the dirty business.

THE SCANDALMONGER

It was a different affair in 1833, when bribery had given place to conscience. Then Greville wrote: 'The vote of the night before last against sinecures was carried in a thin house, only one cabinet minister present (Althorp).'

The dead hand of racketeering has always held a grip difficult to pry loose, and the story of this apparently hopeless transition, from bribery to Victorian responsibility, was among the interesting features of the period. The example and efforts of three people, George III, Fox and Wilkes, have been variously cited by their partisans, as having contributed to it.

George III was a confusing character. On the one hand there were the accounts of his simplicity, kindness, garrulousness and interest in the construction of dumplings as Farmer George, accounts due to the partiality of middle-class writers like Fanny Burney and Dr. Johnson, who were dazzled by the royal condescension; on the other hand there was the historian's picture, due to G. O. Trevelyan, in which he figured as a Machiavel. Trevelyan was prejudiced by his partiality for Fox. The true position probably was that George was a good, conscientious, obstinate and narrow-minded man-of-business, who was determined to follow his mother's advice and to 'be a king'. Such was his industry in the work of government that he was compelled to date his letters to ministers not only by the date, but also by the hour and minute, and he had reason to consider that the salvation of public decency in administration depended upon himself. Whoever his official ministers might be, they were bound by the circumstances of the age to be plunged to the neck in the mire of bribery and place-hunting,

BRIBERY AND CORRUPTION

so that it was impossible to know what ties of disingenuous interest might be behind their measures. The party in power was determined to enjoy the financial fruits of power; that out of it, to seize them. Neither could be expected to improve the situation, for the empty rewards of idealism. George knew that he himself was abstemious, economical and above the scramble: that whatever the fortunes he might expend in patronage, he would personally remain contented with his barley-water and with the society of his astonishing seraglio. He may well have argued that he was the only man in the kingdom who could be relied upon to act from conscience instead of from interest, and the only one who could hope to correct the venality of public servants. He was avaricious for power, not for money; he had inherited the corrupt system perfected but not invented by the great Sir Robert Walpole, and could see no means of reforming it except personally, by prerogative. Unfortunately, his mind was not acute enough to perceive that corruption would have to be countered by principle. He chose the only means that he was able to recognize in the general dishonesty, and attempted to purge the Augean stables with a dirty broom — to counter the corruption of others by his own corruption, which he felt to be dictated by high motives. In short, he could imagine no way to put down bribery except by draining the power of its direction into his own control, and for that he needed to bribe. 'You see my situation,' said he. 'This trade of politics is a rascally business. It is a trade for a scoundrel, and not for a gentleman.'

George set himself to correct the rascals by creating

THE SCANDALMONGER

a party of his own, the King's Friends, who would vote as he directed. There was a mass of crown patronage, consisting of places in the Household, commissions in the forces and similar rewards. With these and the Secret Service money, of which he resumed the administration, he proceeded to bribe a corps d'élite. The result was that there were now three parties in parliament: the ministry, the opposition and the King's Friends. Nor did the King have any hesitation in directing his own party to vote against his own ministry. He proved to be as able in bribery as Walpole himself had been. This might have been well enough if he had confined his efforts to achieving a responsible and incorrupt ministry, but he used the lever to forward other opinions of his own, the only opinions which he felt he could trust, and ended by losing America, and nearly Ireland, in the blind stubbornness of a stupid and well-meaning man. In any case, the inherent fallacy of his position was that it was impossible to correct corruption by corruption, and it is difficult to believe that the efforts of this monarch had any beneficent influence on the growth of the Victorian sense of parliamentary honour.

The claim of Charles James Fox to be regarded as the initiator of this sense seems to be based upon the fact that he was among the first powerful statesmen to go into opposition voluntarily and on principle, without waiting until the wilderness should be thrust upon him. But he was by no means the first politician who sacrificed office to conscience — for instance, there had been Conway and Barré — nor was he the first to deny himself the fruits of power. The great Chatham had refused to take the customary profits from

BRIBERY AND CORRUPTION

the office of Paymaster, an office from which Charles's father was still earning his soubriquet as 'the public defaulter of unaccounted millions'. At the same time, Fox did, after 1774, pursue a parliamentary line which was based on motives of the heart rather than on those of the pocket — or even, like the King's, on those of power — and the generosity of his disinterested nature must have had an effect upon the future of the legislature.

It was to his father Lord Holland, the 'public defaulter', that Fox owed his charming character. Lord Holland seems to have been the kindest and most tolerant of fathers in the history of the eighteenth century, or perhaps of any other, and his 'defaults' were largely due to circumstances outside his control. Public moneys remained in his hands for scandalous periods, but, on the other hand, so did the accounts for which they were to pay remain in the hands of others, unaudited and unpresented. In private life, and in his loving letters, he was the most amiable of mortals. 'Never mind,' he said, when Lady Holland was complaining of some childish fault in Charles. 'He is a sensible little fellow, and will learn to cure himself.' 'Let nothing be done to break his spirit. The world will do that business fast enough.' And, when the child declared that he was going to smash his own watch, 'Well!' said the equanimous father, 'if you must, I suppose you must.' He protected the schoolboy to the best of his ability from the sadism of the period, encouraging him to enjoy the amateur theatricals and other interests which appealed to his young heart. He referred to him in letters, how wisely and affectionately, as 'a little animal'. He took him to France when he was still at Eton, introduced him to the gaming tables, and carefully chose him his first mistress, a dependable one. He had paid his debts to the amount of £140,000 before he was twenty-five. Throughout their association he never complained of a fault, though he rejoiced in every success, and he was repaid by the complete devotion of the three sons who survived childhood, for he was as kind to Ste and to the Squeaker as he was to Charles. Perhaps the most unbelievable feature of their relationship was that Lord Holland never attempted to dictate or to influence conduct. The first mistress was probably the only thing he ever chose for Charles, and of her the boy soon grew tired, asking to return to Eton, which he was immediately allowed to do. There he was flogged.

The result of this extraordinary education was that a politician was launched upon the Age of Scandal who possessed a trusting and a hopeful heart. Whether as a young buck gambling in scarlet heels and blue powder, or as a corpulent and untidy gentleman of middle age, with bushy eyebrows and pendulous nose and heavy lips, Fox was the centre of affection, and a perfect example of the Montessori system. The bitter phrase of Junius about the 'unaccounted millions' makes a poor epitaph for Lord Holland, when one considers the effect of this phenomenon upon the parliamentary history of Britain. He himself would probably have liked to be remembered simply as the father of Charles, who, in later life, when asked why he had forgiven an enemy, was able to say with truth, 'Ah, well, I was always a poor hater.'

Fox was in parliament at the age of twenty, and in

office, as a Lord of the Admiralty, at twenty-one. His early years, as was to be expected, were a series of blunders. He was still kicking up his heels, still losing his fabulous sums at hazard, still enjoying his parliamentary speeches for their debater's points and for their theatrical effect, for he was devoted to acting. He was a success with the shallow, he was unusually well read, and he made speeches almost every night, generally upon the wrong and illiberal side of the question. Even when he first resigned office, at twenty-three, it was more upon a personal pique, and perhaps to some extent as a gambler's throw, than upon any objection in principle against the Royal Marriage Bill. 'That young man,' said the King, not without reason, 'has so thoroughly cast off every principle of common honour and honesty that he must soon become as contemptible as he is odious.'

By the time he was thirty, however, the exuberance of youth had begun to settle. He was always, to insanity, a gambler, throwing away his money almost as if he relished to rid himself of what his father was said to have unfairly earned. He was equally ready to throw away office. Consequently, when this contempt for the *nerfs-de-la-guerre* was joined to the warm trust in humanity which his father had bred in him, he was the very man to resign for disinterested reasons of the heart. It became his destiny to give up his 'places' voluntarily, in defence of the rights of men, just as he gave up his money and his inherited acres at the gaming table. Almost for the first time in English history, a powerful politician was going into the waste lands of opposition of his own accord, for **reasons of personal honour to friends like Rockingham,**

THE SCANDALMONGER

or because he was a champion on principle of the American colonists, or of the exploited natives of India, or of the freedom of the Press. Nearly all the sympathies of his later years were those sympathies of human decency which have commended themselves to the liberal mind. He opposed the slave trade, championed Ireland, rejoiced at the fall of the Bastille and upheld the rights of Catholics. In short, he chose his position from conscience, not from interest. Such generosity rapidly brought him into collision with the King's policy of corruption, however high the King's motives, and Fox at any rate had enough sagacity to perceive that the royal attempts at purgation could never be successful when pursued by dirty means. He did not perceive that his own standards of conduct were idealistically in advance of his time, and consequently, however much his idealism may have changed the future of parliamentary thought, his life reads on the whole as one of failure in the House. In comparison with the more hard-headed Pitt, his periods in office were few and brief. On the other hand, his posthumous influence exceeded Pitt's.

'He was perfectly good-natured,' wrote William Hunt, 'eager, warm-hearted and unselfish. With great natural abilities, a singular quickness of apprehension, and a retentive memory, he combined the habit of doing all things with his might. He was, as he said, a "very painstaking man", and even when Secretary of State wrote copies for a writing-master to improve his handwriting. He delighted in literature and art, his critical faculty was acute, and his taste cultivated. Poetry was to him "the best thing after all", and he declared that he loved "all the poets". He had already acquired a considerable store of learning, and the works of his favourite authors, Greek, Latin, English, French, Italian, and in his later years Spanish, never failed to afford him refreshment and, when he needed it, consolation. He was fond of exercise, and even after he had become very fat retained his activity; he played cricket and tennis well, loved hunting, racing and shooting, and was a good walker and swimmer.' He eventually married his mistress, Mrs. Abingdon, with whom his relations were always delightful, and he had an illegitimate son who was deaf and dumb. The boy died at fifteen, to his intense grief. He himself died of dropsy at the age of fifty-eight. According to Greville, he was 'no believer in religion', but allowed prayers to be read at his death-bed to content his wife, and 'paid little attention to the ceremony'.

If George had any effect upon the morals of parliament by his fuddled conscientiousness, or Fox by his warm heart, the influence of Wilkes was purely logical. Held up to the deepest odium or to the wildest approbation as a radical Jacobin or as a friend of the people, he was in fact a tidy-minded, pertinacious and unambitious person, who saw the logics of one question and insisted on having the right answer. He, like Fox, believed in the principle of the freedom of the Press, but, if that had been his only belief, he would have been remembered for No. 45 of the *North Briton* no more than Fox is remembered for the same belief. Fortunately, the House of Commons decided to turn him out of itself as a result of the quarrel, and Wilkes perceived that this was constitutionally impossible. The House was a collection of representatives elected by the people, he had been elected by the people, and

THE SCANDALMONGER

any talk of his exclusion from parliament was therefore a contradiction in terms. It was a monstrosity, a snake swallowing its own tail. On this simple problem in logics, which was quite abstract and consequently had nothing to do with bribery or sinecures, was fought the chief political battle of the eighteenth century, and its influence was unbounded because it was abstract. No financial reward was attached to it, no bribery could affect it once the reasoning faculty of man had been aroused, and consequently it served to concentrate attention on the new-fangled ideas of Right and Wrong as matters which existed in pure reason, and not in reference to the nearest sinecure.

The story of Wilkes's long and magnificent battle for the recognition of his plain theorem, that representatives of the people could not exclude representatives of the people without ceasing to be representatives of the people, is unfortunately too extensive for a superficial survey. It tore England in two; it terrified George; it set the city and the parliament at one another's throats, so that magistrates and members were busy to commit each other to prison; it compelled Wilkes to fight bloody and almost fatal duels; it drove him into exile, into custody and into Lord Mayor's processions; it raised mobs howling for 'Wilkes and Liberty'; it bothered a harmless letter-writer so much that he began one of his letters with the words: 'Dear Sir, I take the Wilkes and liberty to inform you . . .' In the end, when he had won the victory, he might have made himself the prime minister, or perhaps even a revolutionary dictator, they said, by raising a finger. He did not raise it, and never had intended to do so. He was no demagogue, and explained in later life that he had never been a Wilkesite. He had only been a cultured, brave and resourceful gentleman, who had insisted that two and two made four, and, when that position had been yielded to him, he was content to retire into the country and to read Horace — or perhaps Petronius.

Wilkes had an atrocious squint and no middle-class morals. He was the son of a city magnate, was educated at a private school and at Leyden, and early became a member of the notorious club called the Franciscans, or Monks of Medmenham Abbey. Sir Francis Dashwood, according to Wraxall, 'had founded a society denominated, from his own name, the Franciscans'. Over the doorway of their abbey was inscribed the quotation from Rabelais: 'Fayce que voudrais', and within it were performed a number of orgies by the youthful members, which were probably more scandalous in their intention than in fact. Wilkes himself is said to have let loose a baboon, dressed as the Devil, which he had concealed in a neighbouring room, while their communion was being celebrated, and scared the acolytes. It was afterwards adopted as the 'mysterious object of their homage'. The main activity seems to have been potation, with the eighteenth-century equivalent of the vulgar limerick, and it was to amuse their fellow monks that either Wilkes or else a rake called Thomas Potter wrote a parody of Pope's *Essay on Man*. It was called *The Essay on Woman*, was dedicated to a notorious strumpet, and purported to contain notes by Bishop Warburton. The poem was blasphemous and indecent, containing an obscene parody of the *Veni, Creator Spiritus*, and the dozen copies were at any rate printed by Wilkes, on his private press. It contributed largely to the uproar between Liberty and the House of Commons.

Wilkes was married when under age to a woman ten years his senior, who had a great fortune and greater expectations. His gambling and extravagance quickly ruined her, and they were separated after having one daughter. He became a Fellow of the Royal Society at twenty-two, High Sheriff of Buckinghamshire at twenty-seven, M.P. for Aylesbury at thirty, and Lord Mayor of London at forty-seven. He was intrepid as a duellist, though never the challenger, and lived to be seventy after a life of alternate exile and acclamation, without losing his head in either. At thirty-seven he was touring the Continent with a courtesan 'in whom he discovered all the charms of the Medicean Venus', and he had two natural children besides the legitimate daughter, to whom he was tenderly attached. The only constant feature of his life was debt, and he died, after having contrived to live in luxury, insolvent. His later years were passed, with the steadiness and modesty which had carried him on a level keel through the greatest storms of the century, in reading the classics, in translating Anacreon, and in producing fine editions like his sumptuous Catullus. A man of such wit and good-humour that even Dr. Johnson had found it impossible to quarrel with him, he seems to have possessed little of George's conscience or of Fox's heart, except towards his daughter, and his contribution to the Victorian reform was the lawyer's mind. His was the attitude that constitutional questions must either be right or wrong.

These three men started three different impulses

BRIBERY AND CORRUPTION

which ended in the Reform Bill. Probably the opinion of Tolstoi is the correct one, however, that France produced Napoleon, not Napoleon France. Probably it is true that Hitler was the servant of Germany, not her master, and that it is useless to seek for one or even for several men who have been able to alter the direction of the millions who choose to submit to their government. George, Fox and Wilkes were, after all, only a trio in the general movement. Chatham himself, the Great Commoner, had refused the profits of Paymaster, had said, 'I know that I can save this country and that nobody else can', and had tried, but failed, to rule without corruption. The younger Pitt, the misogynist, was perhaps as disinterested as Fox or as acute as Wilkes, and he was an honourable man. 'My ambition', he once said, 'is character, not office.' Many others had a shoulder at the wheel. But the fact remains that, in the earlier part of the Age of Scandal, Horace Walpole had written: 'Esteem is no principle of union. When men are paid they must vote for what they are bidden to vote' while, when the Age was nearly over, Samuel Romilly could say:

When I was a young man, a seat in parliament was offered me. It was offered in the handsomest manner imaginable: no condition whatever annexed to it: I was told that I was to be quite independent, and was to vote and act just as I thought proper. I could not, however, relieve myself from the apprehension that . . . the person to whom I owed the seat would consider me, without perhaps being quite conscious of it himself, as *his* representative in parliament . . . I weighed the offer very maturely, and in the end I rejected it . . . the little talents which I possessed could never be exerted with any advantage to the public, or any credit to myself, unless I came into parliament quite independent, and answerable for my conduct to God and to my country alone.

So conscientious had members of parliament become by the days of the Reform Bill that they became afflicted by an epidemic of suicide. Paull, Whitbread, Romilly and Castlereagh took their own lives, under the pressure of living up to the Victorian standard of legislative honour.

CHAPTER TWELVE

Sherry

As I may not have another opportunity [wrote Creevey, while considering old times] of committing to paper what little I have of perfect recollection of what Sheridan told me in our walks at Brighton respecting his early life, and as he certainly was a very extraordinary man, I may as well insert it here.
He was at school at Harrow, and, as he told me, never had any scholastic fame while he was there. He said he was a very low-spirited boy, much given to crying when alone, and he attributed this very much to being neglected by his father, to his being left without money, and often not taken home at the regular holidays. From Harrow he went to live in John Street, out of Soho Square, whether with his father or some other instructor, I forget, but he dwelt upon the two years he spent there as those in which he acquired all the reading and learning he had upon any subject.
At the end of this time his father determined to open a kind of academy at Bath — the masters or instructors to be Sheridan the father, his eldest son Charles, and our Sheridan, who was to be *rhetorical usher*. According to his account, however, the whole concern was presently laughed off the stage, and then Sheridan described his happiness as beginning. He danced with all the women at Bath, wrote sonnets and verses in praise of some, satires and lampoons upon others, and in a very short time became the established wit and fashion of the place.
It was at this period of his life he fell in love with Miss Lindley, whom he afterwards married, but she

was carried off by her father at that time to a convent in France, to be kept out of his way. Then it was he became embroiled with Mr. Mathews, who was likewise a lover of Miss Lindley, as well as her libeller. Sheridan fought two duels with Mr. Mathews upon this subject, both times with swords. The first time was in some hotel or tavern in Henrietta St., Covent Garden, when Mathews was disarmed and begged his life. Upon Mr. Mathews's return to Bath, Sheridan used his triumph with so little moderation, that Mr. Mathews left Bath to live in Wales; but soon he was induced to believe that he had compromised his honour by quitting Bath and leaving his reputation at the mercy of Sheridan. Accordingly, a messenger arrived from him to Sheridan, with a written certificate of Mathews's undoubted honour in the former affair, to be *signed* by Sheridan, or else the messenger was to deliver him a second challenge.

Sheridan preferred the latter course of proceeding, and the duel was fought at King's Weston (if I recollect right). According to Sheridan's account, never was anything so desperate. Sheridan's sword broke in a point blank thrust into Mathews's chest; upon which he closed, and they both fell, Mathews uppermost; but, in falling, his sword broke likewise, sticking into the earth and snapping. However, he drew the sharp end out of the ground, and with this he stabbed Sheridan in the face and body, over and over again, till it was thought he must die. Sheridan named both the seconds, but I forget them. He said they were both cut for ever afterwards for not interfering. He said, likewise, there was a regular proceeding before the Mayor of Bristol, on the ground that Mr. Mathews had worn some kind of armour to protect him, which broke Sheridan's sword . . . Sheridan was taken to some hotel at Bath, where his life for some time was despaired of, but . . . he rallied and recovered.

He then lived for some time at Waltham Cross, and

UNCORKING OLD SHERRY

was in bad health, but used to steal up to town to see and hear Miss Lindley in publick, though he was under an engagement with her family not to pursue her any more in private. At length, however, they met, and eventually were married. Miss Lindley's reputation at this time was so great, that her engagements for the year were £5000. This resource, however, Sheridan would not listen to her receiving any longer, altho' he himself had not a single farthing. He said she might sing to oblige the King or Queen, but to receive money while she was his wife was quite out of the question. Upon which old Lindley, her father, said this might do very well for him — Mr. Sheridan — but that for him — Mr. Lindley — it was a very hard case; that his daughter had always been a very good daughter to him, and very generous to him out of the funds she gained by her profession, and that it was very hard upon him to be cut off all at once from this supply. This objection was disposed of by Sheridan in the following manner.
Miss Lindley had £3000 of her own, of which Sheridan gave her father £2000. With the remaining £1000, the only fortune Mr. and Mrs. Sheridan began the world with, he took a cottage at Slough, where they lived, he said, most happily, a gig and horse being their principal luxury, with a man to look after both the master and his horse. But by the end, or before the end, of the year, the £1000 was drawing rapidly to a finish, and then it was that Sheridan thought of play-writing as a pecuniary resource, and he wrote *The Rivals*. Having got an introduction to the theatre, he took his play there, and finally was present to see it acted, but would not let Mrs. Sheridan come up from Slough for the same purpose. *The Rivals*, upon its first performance, was *damned*; when Sheridan got to Slough and told his wife of it she said: 'My dear Dick, I am delighted. I always knew it was impossible you could make anything by writing

plays; so now there is nothing left for it but my beginning to sing publickly again, and we shall have as much money as we like.'

'No,' said Sheridan, 'that shall never be. I see where the fault was; the play was too long, and the parts were badly cast.'

So he altered and curtailed the play, and had address or interest enough to get the parts newly cast. At the expiration of six weeks it was acted again, with unbounded applause. His fame as a dramatick writer was settled from that time. When it was he became proprietor of Drury Lane Theatre, or how it was accomplished, I did not learn from him, but it was the only property he ever possessed, and, with the commonest discretion on his part, would have made him a most affluent man.

Sheridan's talents, displayed in his plays, procured him very shortly both male and *female* admirers among the higher orders. The families of Lord Coventry and Lord Harrington he spoke of as his first patrons. When it was he began with politicks, I don't recollect, but he was a great parliamentary reformer the latter end of the American war, and one of a committee of either five or seven (I forget which number) who used to sit regularly at the Mansion House upon this subject.

In 1780, the year of a general election, his object was to get into Parliament if possible, and he was going to make a trial at Wootton-Bassett. The night before he set out, being at Devonshire House and everybody talking about the general election, Lady Cork asked Sheridan about *his* plans, which led to her saying that she had often heard her brother Monckton say he thought an opposition man might come in for Stafford, and that if, in the event of Sheridan failing at Wootton, he liked to try his chance at Stafford, she would give him a letter of introduction to her brother. This was immediately done. Sheridan went to

SHERRY

Wootton-Bassett, where he had not a chance. Then he went to Stafford, produced Lady Cork's letter, offered himself as a candidate, and was elected. For Stafford he was member till 1806 — six-and-twenty years. I remember asking him if he could fix upon any one point of time in his life that was decidedly happier than all the rest, and he said certainly — it was after dinner the day of his first election for Stafford, when he stole away by himself to speculate upon those prospects of distinguishing himself which had been opened to him.
I did not hear any further of his own history from himself. . . .

The Prince of course was delighted with all this [the larks on Madame Gerobtzoff's lap, quoted in *The Age of Scandal*]; but at last Sheridan made himself so ill with drinking, that he came to us soon after breakfast one day, saying he was in a perfect fever, desiring he might have some table beer, and declaring that he would spend that day with us, and send his excuses by Bloomfield for not dining at the Pavilion. I felt his pulse, and found it going tremendously, but instead of beer, we gave him some hot white wine, of which he drank a bottle, I remember, and his pulse subsided almost instantly . . . After dinner that day he must have drunk at least a bottle and a half of wine. In the evening we were all going to the Pavilion, where there was to be a ball, and Sheridan said he would go home i.e., to the Pavilion (where he slept) and would go quietly to bed. He desired me to tell the Prince, if he asked me after him, that he was far from well, and was gone to bed.
So when supper was served at the Pavilion about twelve o'clock, the Prince came up to me and said: 'What the devil have you done with Sheridan today, Creevey? I know he has been dining with you, and I have not seen him the whole day.'

I said he was by no means well and had gone to bed; upon which the Prince laughed heartily, as if he thought it all fudge, and then, taking a bottle of claret and a glass, he put them both in my hands and said: 'Now Creevey, go to his bedside and tell him I'll drink a glass of wine with him, and if he refuses, I admit he must be damned bad indeed.'
I would willingly have excused myself on the score of his being really ill, but the Prince would not believe a word of it, so go I must. When I entered Sheridan's bedroom, he was in bed, and, his great fine eyes being instantly fixed upon me, he said; —
'Come, I see this is some joke of the Prince, and I am not in a state for it.'
I excused myself as well as I could, and as he would not touch the wine, I returned without pressing it, and the Prince seemed satisfied he must be ill.
About two o'clock, however, the supper having been long over, and everybody engaged in dancing, who should I see standing at the door but Sheridan, powdered as white as snow, as smartly dressed as ever he could be from top to toe . . . I joined him and expressed my infinite surprise at this freak of his. He said:
'Will you go with me, my dear fellow, into the kitchen, and let me see if I can find a bit of supper.' Having arrived there, he began to play off his cajolery upon the servants, saying if he was the Prince they should have much better accommodation, &c., &c., so that he was surrounded by supper of all kinds, every one waiting upon him. He ate away and drank a bottle of claret in a minute, returned to the ballroom, and when I left it between three and four he was dancing.

Mrs. Creevey wrote to her daughter in 1806:

I am going to Somerset House to inquire after poor Sheridan, who went from this house very ill at 12

SHERRY

o'clock last night . . . He complained of sore throat and shivering, and his pulse was the most frightful one I ever felt; it was so tumultuous and so strong that when one touched it, it seemed not only to shake his arm, but his whole frame . . . I lighted a fire and a great many candles, and Mr. Creevey, who was luckily just come home from Petty's, began to tell him stories . . . Then we sent for some wine, of which he was so frightened it required persuasion to make him drink six small glasses, of which the effect was immediate in making him not only happier, but composing his pulse . . . In the midst of his dismals he said most clever, funny things, and at last got to describing Mr. Hare, and others of his old associates, with the hand of a real master, and made one lament that such extraordinary talents should have such numerous alloys. He received a note from Lady Elizabeth Forster, with a good account of Mr. Fox. It ended with — 'try to drink less and speak the truth'. He was very funny about it and said: 'By G—d! I speak more truth than *she* does, however.'

Sheridan's was a life to which legends adhered. Newspapers claimed, and biographers repeated, that he had died in actual want and that he had been arrested in his coffin. Stories of his raking with the Regent and of the deceptions which he was said to have practised on his creditors were told and exaggerated. The fact was that he was so extraordinary a person that the mind found difficulty in grasping his scale — with the result that any tale could stick to him, and no exaggeration seemed too strange. It will have been noticed, however, that six small glasses of wine were sufficient to elevate his genius, and it was probably so with many of his excesses: his debts were less than Pitt's, and were, unlike Pitt's, paid by his own family: he was not arrested in his coffin. At the same time, it does seem difficult to believe that so tipsy a figure, and one who remained in debt — though only once in a sponging house — throughout the latter part of his life, should have written the two great comedies of the English language; that he should have efficiently filled the offices of Under-secretary for Foreign Affairs, Secretary to the Treasury, Treasurer to the Navy, Privy Councillor and chief adviser to the future King; and that he should have been the manager and proprietor of Drury Lane Theatre, beside being a member of parliament who could deliver a speech of nearly six hours after which 'the whole house — the members, peers and strangers — involuntarily joined in a tumult of applause, and adopted a mode of expressing their approbation, new and irregular in that house, by loudly and repeatedly clapping their hands'. Perhaps the explanation may have lain in Creevey's picture of the Pavilion evening: in the endurance of that pale, powdered and indomitable figure, who had had the bottom to rise again and to force himself back to the revels, however ill he felt.

Much of Sheridan's life was spent in resurrection. He was born in Dublin in 1751, left Ireland before he was nine, was educated as Creevey tells, wrote *The Rivals* at the age of twenty-four and *The School for Scandal* at twenty-six, was elected at that early age to Dr. Johnson's brilliant Club, was in parliament at twenty-nine and in office at thirty-one. It was typical of his period that he should have written when young, 'I am determined to gain all the knowledge that I can bring within my reach. I will make myself as much master as I can of French and Italian.' It was typical, too, that he should have been able to quote Greek in the Commons. He was a Whig, a politician of liberal mind, and his tenures of office were consequently short. He was Secretary to the Treasury for less than a year, before the ministry was dismissed, leaving him to rise again. Even in family life, he had to recover from disasters: from the death of his first wife, and from the consumption of his eldest son. He was making £10,000 a year from Drury Lane when it had to be pulled down: he exceeded the estimated cost of rebuilding by £75,000. Fifteen years later the new theatre, his main property, was burned to the ground. It was then, they said, that he sat in the street with a bottle of wine to view the conflagration, explaining that if a man could not be comfortable at his own fireside then he did not know where he could be comfortable. He was so much respected and admired that the House of Commons adjourned on that occasion, as if the burning of Drury Lane had been equivalent to the death of royalty.

Sheridan suffered from insomnia and from the fits of toxic depression so common in his century; his volatility was too great to be maintained. He may have taken to his claret, and in later life to his brandy, as a tonic. He was said to have died a water-drinker. He was buried in Westminster Abbey in 1816, and a Mrs. Parkhurst wrote: 'He took away with him a thousand charitable actions, a heart in which there was no hard part, a spirit free from envy and malice, and he is gone in the undiminished brightness of his talent, gone before pity had withered admiration.' He left behind one remark which bore upon the legends which have clung to him: 'It is a fact that I have scarcely

ever in my life contradicted one calumny against me
... I have since on reflection ceased to approve my
own conduct in these respects. Were I to lead my life
over again, I should act otherwise.'

Perhaps there had been no literary figure of Sheridan's stature in England, who had excelled in so many fields of effort. Shakespeare had written better plays, but he had never been a statesman and a politician: Bacon had been a politician and an author, but never a business man who had managed the national theatre. Sheridan, greater than Bacon, had been given the opportunity, but had refused it, 'to hide his head in a coronet'.

The puzzling feature of this character, in such an age and with such a career, was that he seemed to everybody to be honest in politics — if not always so to his creditors. There was a feeling that, in such a meteor, there ought to have been the duplicity of a Bacon or of a Brougham; or that there ought to have been some tragic collapse — perhaps with the suicide which became common among politicians at the beginning of the nineteenth century. Considering his drunken frolics under heavy strain, he ought to have been a traitor like Rigby and the rest of them. But he remained a jovial figure called Sherry, who accomplished prodigies without seeming to do so, who solved the problems of his correspondence by seldom opening letters, who contrived to weather the tempest of his existence for sixty-five years, and who would have assisted his biographers if he had not been too good-natured to contradict the calumnies. They were left to finger stray quotations, from the remarks of dependable contemporaries like Creevey, and to wonder what on earth it was that had set him going, or what he was, or why he was so.

Horace Walpole thought him a prodigy, and also honourable. 'What merit is there in pains, study, and application, compared with the extreme abilities of such men as . . . Mr. Sheridan?' 'I have never heard anything to give me suspicions of his behaving unhandsomely.' Byron described an evening with him, in old age.

Yesterday, I dined out with a large-ish party, where there were Sheridan and Colman, Harry Harris of Covent Garden, and his brother, Sir Gilbert Heathcote, Douglas Kinnaird, and others, of note and notoriety. Like other parties of the kind, it was first silent, then talky, then argumentative, then disputatious, then unintelligible, then altogethery, then inarticulate, and then drunk. When we had reached the last step of this glorious ladder, it was difficult to get down again without stumbling; and, to crown all, Kinnaird and I had to conduct Sheridan down a damned corkscrew staircase, which had certainly been constructed before the discovery of fermented liquors, and to which no legs, however crooked, could possibly accommodate themselves. We deposited him safe at home, where his man, evidently used to the business, waited to receive him in the hall.

Both he and Colman were, as usual, very good; but I carried away much wine, and the wine had previously carried away my memory; so that all was hiccup and happiness for the last hour or so, and I am not impregnated with any of the conversation. Perhaps you heard of a late answer of Sheridan to the watchman who found him bereft of that 'divine particle of air', called reason ***. He, the watchman, found Sherry in the street, fuddled and bewildered, and almost insensible. 'Who are *you*, sir?' — no answer.

THE SCANDALMONGER

'What's your name?' — a hiccup. 'What's your name?' — Answer, in a slow, deliberate and impassive tone — 'Wilberforce ! ! !' Is not that Sherry all over? — and, to my mind, excellent. Poor fellow, *his* very dregs are better than the 'first sprightly runnings' of others. My paper is full, and I have a grievous headache.

When the prodigy was dead, the same noble author wrote to Moore:

In writing the *Life* of Sheridan, never mind the angry lies of the humbug Whigs. Recollect that he was an Irishman and a clever fellow, and that *we* have had some very pleasant days with him. Dont forget that he was at school at Harrow, where, in my time, we used to shew his name — R. B. Sheridan, 1765 — as an honour to the walls . . . Depend upon it there were worse folks going, of that gang [the Regent's friends], than ever Sheridan was.

CHAPTER THIRTEEN

Pure Grim Devils

AFTER more than a century of thrillers, it is difficult for people to look back to sedater days when there were only novels called *Evelina* or *Cecilia*, and not too many of those. In 1820, however, the still vivacious Mrs. Piozzi, who had got into hot water with the *ton* for ceasing to be Dr. Johnson's Mrs. Thrale, but who was still going strong at the age of eighty all the same, wrote to her old friend Fanny Burney — who had been forced to forgive the other's lapse after falling into similar errors by becoming Madame D'Arblay. It amused the two old bluestockings to remember.

'How changed', exclaimed the octogenarian, 'is the taste of verse, prose and painting! since *le bon vieux temps*, dear Madam! Nothing attracts us but what terrifies, and is within — *if* within — a hair's breadth of positive disgust . . . Some of the strange things they *write* remind me of Squoire Richard's visit to the Tower Menagerie, when he says "Odd, they are *pure grim devils*" — particularly a wild and hideous tale called Frankenstein.'

Horace Walpole's Castle of Otranto, with its mail gauntlets on the banisters, supernatural helms as big as hansom cabs and pictures which walked out of their frames — but all, and how indignant Horry would have been to hear us say so, possessing that charming tincture of the ridiculous which was one of the essences of Strawberry Hill — had started something — long before Mary Shelley — which would eventually branch into Poe and Le Fanu, into Dracula and the Penny Dreadful and Edgar Wallace and into all the shockers on the twentieth-century library shelves.

Frankenstein, to the not unrelished *frisson* of Dr. Johnson's belle, was the first to step from the old Gothick to the new Horror. That eight-foot Monster, which had been assembled and given the breath of life by a Swiss philosopher, Mr. Frankenstein; that Being created eight feet high because it was easier to manufacture some of the smaller parts when slightly enlarged; that fearsome Figure with contorted, mummy-like muscles and creaking gait — a mere journeyman piece — is still a genuine shock in 1951. It would make the grade without difficulty for the latest tabloid strip in America, and probably has done so, long ago. Probably it is on the cinema too, with Boris Karloff in the title role — but if so it will be with this one singular difference, that the monster itself is nowadays called Frankenstein, while its builder has become anonymous. Such is the revenge which the public takes on mediocrity. Mary Shelley's philosopher was a bore: a mixture, one suspects, of Byron and Shelley — and what mixture could be more boring if it happened the wrong way round? Her nameless Giant was more interesting than its master, and it has consequently captured the only name they owned between them.

The excitement took place — the birth of the Shocker did — on a wet evening in 1816, in Switzerland, when Byron, Shelley, Mary Shelley and Polidori began talking about ghost stories in general. They decided to write one each, in a kind of competition.

TALES OF WONDER

PURE GRIM DEVILS

Shelley lost interest, Byron was delivered of a fragment of Mazeppa, Polidori thought of a lady who only had a skull instead of a head because she would persist in peeping through keyholes — but Mary, who must have seemed the least of the competitors, after much travail produced the first modern horror story.

It was not very modern either. We are accustomed by so long a procession of Wilkie Collinses, Conan Doyles, Wellses, Sayerses and the rest of them, to the stabbed millionaire in the library, to the potion of curare, to the Robot or to the Tarzan, to the corpse dissolved in the tank of acid, that we demand a high standard of apparent accuracy in facts. We know how long a body ought to stay warm, and we are not willing to be fobbed off with inaccuracies, or with coincidences in detail. We pounce upon the quarter-chimes in the alibi like hawks. Our Robots must work, our Tarzans must live in a particular part of Africa, and anybody not killed with a neat intravenous injection of air-bubbles scarcely counts as dead. Mary Shelley did not care for all this. How people got to the North Pole, or how they lived on nuts and berries when these were out of season, or how they could exist for many months in the woodshed of a cottage without being noticed by the cottagers, such were matters of indifference to her. Consequently it is difficult to read the original *Frankenstein* because of the puerilities of fact. We have developed in that direction. But in another direction, perhaps we have much receded from the standards of the first thrilleress.

Mary Shelley took her miserable villain seriously. She tried to enter into its rights and character. No American tabloid strip would do so now. The 'Frankenstein' would now be mechanized, Mars-ified, armoured, awful, would be the evil principle of the piece. It would be overcome in the end, by the pre-potent, big-business hero and by the nubile mother-heroine, without anybody caring a fig whether it had possessed any rights or any feelings of its own. Shelley's wife did care, and this is why we read her book. Indeed, there is only one person now, in all the story, who moves our feelings. The Byronic imbecile of a 'natural philosopher' (i.e. biologist) who created the Demon, his tedious and dull-witted friends or relations who are constantly and deservedly butchered when his creation has run amok, none of these are now more interesting than anybody in a novel by Richardson. But the wretched, the half-human, the yellow-skinned, the watery-eyed, the black-lipped, the ill-made Caliban — made so by no fault of his own — the gawky, un-Eve'd Adam begging for a mate — for a hideous one, so that it may come to love even him — the self-sprung character always on the edge of being beautiful — the wild, hoarse voice pleading with ill-fitted tongue that 'I am malicious because I am miserable... Let me see that I excite the sympathy of some existing thing; do not deny me my request!' — this creature, yes, it does still touch our hearts, as, with all its evil done, in terrible remorse, it vanishes towards the North Pole on its raft of ice, and 'is soon borne away by the waves and lost in darkness and distance'.

At eighty years of age, an old lady who had once quelled the snuffy turbulence of Dr. Johnson noticed that pure grim devil with a certain thrill. Eighty years later, in 1900, Poe and Le Fanu were long dead, and the author of the *Island of Dr. Moreau* was already thirty-four.

CHAPTER FOURTEEN

Scandal

'BESIDES,' pronounced Dr. Johnson in the Hebrides, 'I love anecdotes . . . If a man is to wait till he weaves anecdotes into a system, we may be long in getting them, and get but few in comparison of what we might get.'

It was the era of the anecdote, of tittle-tattle for aristocrats, of comical gossip, and, incidentally, of the most brilliant risky stories in the English language. Here, as some slight excuse for dubbing theirs the Age of Scandal, is a collection without system of stories taken mainly from Horace Walpole, Earl of Orford — the most charming, the most gentlemanly and the most cultured of all their tattlers.

A COMPLAISANT RECEPTION

T'other night, a description was given me of the most extraordinary declaration of love that ever was made. Have you seen young Poniatowski? He is very handsome. You have seen the figure of the Duchess of Gordon, who looks like a raw-boned Scotch metaphysician that has got a red face by drinking water. One day at the drawing-room, having never spoken to him, she sent one of the foreign ministers to invite Poniatowski to dinner with her for the next day. He bowed and went. The moment the door opened, her two little sons, attired like Cupids, with bows and arrows, shot at him; and one of them literally hit his hair, and was very near putting his eye out, and hindering his casting it to the couch

Where she, another sea-born Venus, lay.

THE SCANDALMONGER

The only company besides this Highland goddess were two Scotchmen, who could not speak a word of any language but their own Erse; and, to complete his astonishment at this allegorical entertainment, with the dessert there entered a little horse, and galloped round the table; a hieroglyphic I cannot solve. Poniatowski accounts for this profusion of kindness by his great-grandmother being a Gordon; but I believe it is to be accounted for by...

CANVASSING FOR PARLIAMENT

The great cry against Nugent at Bristol was for having voted for the Jew-bill: one old woman said, 'What, must we be represented by a Jew and an Irishman?' He replied with great quickness, 'My good dame, if you step aside with me into a corner, I will show you that I am not a Jew, and that I am an Irishman.'

AN ILL-USED SEA CAPTAIN

Last Monday there was at Court a Sea-Captain who had been made prisoner at Algiers. He was complaining how cruelly he had been used. They asked how? 'Why,' said he, 'you see I am not strong, and could do no hard labour, and so they put me to hatch eggs.' But his greatest grievance was, that, when he had hatched a brood, they took away his chickens. Did you ever hear of a more tender-hearted old hen?

A JACOBEAN TOMB

At two miles from Houghton Park is the mausoleum of the Bruces, where I saw the most ridiculous monument of one of Lady Ailesbury's predecessors that ever was imagined; I beg she will never keep such company. In the midst of an octagon chapel is the tomb of Diana, Countess of Oxford and Elgin. From a huge unwieldy base of white marble rises a black marble cistern; literaly a cistern that would serve for an eating-room. In the midst of this, to the knees, stands her ladyship

SCANDAL

in a white domino or shroud, with her left hand erect as giving her blessing. It put me in mind of Mrs. Cavendish when she got drunk in the bathing-tub.

THE GREAT O

Shall I make you smile, Madam, in this ugly hour? You know my Swiss David's solemnity and uncouth pronunciation, which he thinks perfect. He came into the room t'other day very composedley and dangling his arms said, 'Auh! dar is Meses Ellis want some of your large flags to put in her great O.' — I cried, what! though I could scarce question him for laughing. At last with much ado, I discovered that Mrs. Ellis's wants lay in her grotto.

A USE FOR SCANDAL

An old Duchess of Rutland, mother of the late Duchess of Montrose, whenever a visitor told her some news or scandal, cried to her daughter, 'Lucy, do step into the next room, and make a memorandum of what Lady Greenwich, or Lady M.M. or N.N. has been telling us.' 'Lord! Madam, to be sure it cannot be true.' 'No matter, child; it will do for news into the country.'

A PHILOSOPHIC HUNTSMAN

I have been reading a book as heterogeneous from my pursuits as Mr. Storer's new profession from his — Mr. Beckford's on Hunting; and as I always reckon that any book pays me in which I find one passage that pleases me or tells me something new (I mean that I care to learn, for as to novelty, every book of science could tell me what I don't know), I found one jewel in Mr. Beckford's, for which I would have perused a folio. His Huntsman christened one of his hounds, 'LYMAN'. 'Lyman!' said the squire; 'why, James, what does Lyman mean?' 'Lord, Sir,' said James, 'what does anything mean?' I am transported with James's good sense and philosophy.

THE SCANDALMONGER

IN A WOOD
It was written by the late Lord Melcome, on a Mrs. Strawbridge, whom I know, and who was still a very handsome black woman; she lived at the corner house going to Saville Row, over against the late Duke of Grafton's. The Lord, then Mr. Dodington, fancied himself in love with her, and one day obtained an assignation. He found her laying on a couch. But, whether he had not expected so kind a reception, or was not so impatient to precipitate the conclusion of the romance, he kneeled down, and seizing her hand, cried, 'Oh, that I had you out in a wood!' — 'In a wood,' cried the astonished Statira; 'what would you do? rob me?'

NOW AND THEN A GUARD
Bon-mots come thicker than changes. Charles Townshend, receiving an account of the impression the King's death had made, was told Miss Chudleigh cried. 'What,' said he, 'Oysters?' And last night, Mr. Dauncey, asking George Selwyn if Princess Amelia would have a guard? he replied, 'Now and then one, I suppose.'

LIVELY STATUES
I remember a story of old Thomas, Earl of Pembroke: he one day took it into his grave head to give eyeballs with charcoal to all his statues at Wilton, and then called his wife and daughters to see how much livelier the gods, goddesses, and emperors were grown! Lively, indeed! for Mr. Arundel, his son-in-law, had improved on his Lordship's idea, and with the same charcoal had distributed whole thickets of black hair over the bodies of the whole marble assembly.

REASON FOR SUICIDE
Mr. Williams tells a story of some acquaintance of his

who killed himself and left a note in one of his pockets explaining his motive to have been that he was 'tired of buttoning and unbuttoning'.

GLENBERVIE

WISE MAN'S RELIGION

He said a lady asked the famous Lord Shaftesbury what religion he was of. He answered the religion of wise men. She asked, what was that? He answered, wise men never tell.

EGMONT

A SPORTIVE MONARCH

[Louis XV] seeing the Grand Provost de Sourches in the Garden of Diana, he exclaimed: 'I will give the Grand Provost a good fright,' whereupon he loosed his arrow and hit the Grand Provost in the stomach, but was upset at having been so skilful. The Grand Provost is in a bad way.

MARAIS

THE PIG-FACED LADY

It was generally believed in 1814 that a pig-faced female, 'the daughter of a great lady', resided in Grosvenor Square.

Sir William Elliot [says Gronow], a youthful baronet, calling one day to pay his respects to the great lady in Grosvenor Square, was ushered into a drawing-room, where he found a person fashionably dressed, who, on turning towards him, displayed a hideous pig's face. Sir William, a timid young gentleman, could not refrain from uttering a shout of horror, and rushed to the door in a manner the reverse of polite; when the infuriated lady or animal, uttering a series of grunts, rushed at the unfortunate baronet as he was retreating, and inflicted a severe wound on the back of his neck.

THE SCANDALMONGER

AN ILL WIND

It is an ill wind that blows nobody any good; — so said the Duchess Dowager of Marlborough in a little note which she sent wrapped up with an Ensign's commission to a young gentleman of small fortune, who being present the day before in a large company where her Grace happened to have an unlucky escape, took it up, and ran off with it, as if in great confusion, heartily begging all their pardons.

Gentleman's Magazine for 1777

AN EXACTING GUEST

According to the fencing master Angelo, the eccentric Mr. Cuzzans, during a severe frost,

went into a coffee-room at Bath, dressed in a complete suit of nankeen, ordered a decanter of cold water, which he poured over his head, over his shoulders, and into his shoes. He then called for a cup of coffee, eggs, and spinach, the *Philadelphia Mercury*, two pipes, half a lemon and a Welsh rabbit.

Later, he ordered a boot-jack, a pint of vinegar, a paper of pins, and some barley-sugar, ending with instructions that they should

bring me, after I am in bed, a dish of fried milestones, with a warming-pan, cold without sugar, and I shall be satisfied ... He then opened his portmanteau, which he had brought under his arm, put on six shirts over his suit of nankeen, bowed with great dignity to the company, ordered his bed to be sprinkled with sawdust, and took his leave for the night.

DUCAL GRANDEUR OF OLD Q

After ringing his bell, the servant came into the room, stood some time without the Duke's speaking or looking at him, and then asked if his Grace wanted any-

CI-DEVANT OCCUPATIONS

SCANDAL

thing, who upon that said to him, 'God damn you, am I obliged to tell you what I want?'
GLENBERVIE

DUCAL WITTICISM OF DE CHARTRES
The Duc de Chartres [wrote Lady Harriot Eliot indignantly] wears upon his buttons an intaglio of a horse and a mare in a *gay disposition* which he presents to ye ladies for their inspection.

AN EXAMPLE OF MEIOSIS
Somebody had lent the *Lives of the Twelve Caesars* to a man who was famous for speaking well of everybody, and when he returned the book, asked him what he thought of Nero. He answered, 'Why I must own he *was* a wag.'
GLENBERVIE

AN ENERGETIC PEERESS
The prostitute (referred to in the peerages as 'widow of —— Horton Esq.') who became Lady Maynard was the daughter of a tailor.
I have heard that she would tell some of her intimate friends that in the early part of her life she had once earned, in single guineas, one hundred in one day. Whether she left off *lassata* or *satiata* I know not.
GLENBERVIE

ABSOLUTELY BEAMING
When the Princess of Wales went first to live at Blackheath, Lord and Lady Lavington were invited to dine and sleep there with other company. Lady Sheffield was then in waiting. A double bed was prepared for this couple, which the Princess found caused a deal of discourse among the upper servants. My Lady's maid and my Lord's *valet de chambre* were all terror and alarm. They said their master and

THE SCANDALMONGER

mistress had not slept together for many a year. What was to be done? Her Royal Highness's housekeeper came trembling to represent the case, but stated at the same time that there was no other bed or bedroom unoccupied. Princess: 'Never mind. Take no further notice.' My Lord and my Lady retired after supper, and next morning Lady Lavington came to breakfast *toute rayonnante* and said she had not had so good a night for a vast number of years.

GLENBERVIE

NOT A CIRCULAR

Lady Anne Foley, who according to Lord Glenbervie had a great many gentlemen-friends, wrote to her husband after one of her lyings-in:

Dear Richard, I give you joy — I have just made you the father of a beautiful boy. Yours, etc. PS. — This is not a circular.

JE ME PROMÈNE

The Count de M—— ... was, I am sorry to say, paying an evening visit to a fair lady during her husband's absence, when that gentleman unexpectedly returned and the room having only one door, which was to give ingress to the jealous husband, the gallant gay Lothario, after looking wildly round the room for a hiding place, took refuge in a large old-fashioned clock-case which stood in a corner of the room. There he ensconced himself; and, as his entry stopped the pendulum, he tried with his tongue against his palate to imitate the ticking noise of the clock; hoping that the husband would make a short stay, and that he would be soon released from his uncomfortable situation.

But that gentleman, who had been privately warned by an anonymous letter that all was not right at home, showed no symptoms of moving from the large arm-

chair, just in front of the clock, where he had taken up his position. My unfortunate friend could no longer keep on the clicking noise, — his tongue clove to the roof of his mouth, — and he had to keep silence. The husband arose, crying out to his wife, '*Chère amie*, the clock is stopped: I must wind it up.' Before the lady could arrest his progress, he had opened the door and found the young Lovelace tightly wedged in. 'What are you doing there, you villain?' shouted the enraged husband. '*Je me promène*,' replied the young man.
GRONOW

ALL A SURPRISE
Lady Salisbury is said by the scandalous chronicle to have had a child by a Mr. Hales of Hertfordshire. A gentleman was saying one day near the time when that report was most current, to her bosom friend, the Dowager Lady Essex, that he wondered Lady Salisbury could have *liked* so plain and vulgar a man, when her friend Lady Essex replied, 'That is all a mistake. She never liked him. It was a mere surprise. They had been hunting (a diversion Lady Salisbury was formerly much addicted to). The chase was long and Hales being accidentally up with Lady Salisbury when it was over, they returned home together in a back chaise. So you see it was all a surprise.'
GLENBERVIE

CHAPTER FIFTEEN

A Troublesome Cargo — More Noise than Danger

IN 1788, at the age of thirty-three, a hearty young mariner called John Nicol joined his ship in the river of London. The *Lady Julian* was a convict ship, destined to carry 245 female malefactors to transportation in New South Wales, and the mariner Nicol was a handy fellow, whose proper trade was that of a ship's cooper. But on this occasion he signed as steward.

Being a cooper, however, it fell to Nicol's lot to strike off the irons of the lady convicts as they came aboard. 'There were not a great many very bad characters,' he wrote at the end of his life, 'the greater number were for petty crimes, and a great proportion for being disorderly, that is, street-walkers; the colony at the time being in great want of women.'

Among his clients at the anvil, for whom he was paid 2/6 a time, there was 'a Scottish girl who broke her heart', 'Mrs. Barnsley, a noted sharper and shoplifter (who) had a brother a highwayman, who often came to see her, as well dressed and genteel in his appearance as any gentleman', 'Mrs. Davis, a noted swindler', 'one Mary Williams, transported for receiving stolen goods', 'Sarah Dorset (who) had not been protected by the villain that ruined her above six weeks', 'Mrs. Nelly Kerwin, a female of daring habits',

A TROUBLESOME CARGO

'Nance Farrel' — of whom more anon, 'Mary Rose, a timid modest girl (for perjury)' and, above all, there was Sarah Whitelam.

When we were fairly out at sea, every man on board took a wife from among the convicts, they nothing loath. The girl with whom I lived, for I was as bad in this point as the others, was named Sarah Whitelam. She was a native of Lincoln, a girl of a modest reserved turn, as kind and true a creature as ever lived. I courted her for a week and upwards, and would have married her upon the spot, had there been a clergyman on board. She had been banished for a mantle she had borrowed from an acquaintance ... and she was transported for seven years. I had fixed my fancy upon her from the moment I knocked the rivet out of her irons upon my anvil, and as firmly resolved to bring her back to England, my lawful wife, as ever I did intend anything in my life. She bore me a son in our voyage out. What is become of her, whether she is alive or dead, I know not. That I do not is no fault of mine, as my narrative will show. But to proceed. We soon found that we had a troublesome cargo, yet not dangerous or very mischievous, as I may say more noise than danger.

When any of them, such as Nance Farrel, who was ever making disturbance, became very troublesome, we confined them down in the hold, and put on the hatch. This, we were soon convinced, had no effect, as they became in turns outrageous, on purpose to be confined. Our agent and the captain wondered at the change in their behaviour. I, as steward, found it out by accident. As I was overhauling the stores in the hold, I came upon a hogshead of bottled porter, with a hole in the side of it, and, in place of full, there were nothing but empty bottles in it. Another was begun, and more than a box of candles had been carried off. I immediately told the captain, who now found out the cause of the late insubordination, and desire of confinement. We were forced to change the manner of punishing them. I was desired by the agent, Lieutenant Edgar, who was an old lieutenant of Cook's, to take a flour barrel, and cut a hole in the top for their head, and one on each side for their arms. This we called a wooden jacket. Next morning Nance Farrel, as usual, came to the door of the cabin, and began to abuse the agent and captain. They desired her to go away between decks, and be quiet. She became worse in her abuse, wishing to be confined, and sent to the hold; but, to her mortification, the jacket was produced, and two men brought her upon deck, and put it on. She laughed and capered about for a while, and made light of it. One of her comrades lighted a pipe, and gave it her. She walked about strutting and smoking the tobacco, and making the others laugh at the droll figure she made; she walked a minuet, her head moving from side to side like a turtle. The agent was resolved she should be heartily tired, and feel in all its force the disagreeableness of her present situation. She could only walk or stand, to sit or lie down was out of her power. She began to get weary, and begged to be released. The agent would not, until she asked his pardon, and promised amendment in future. This she did in humble terms before evening, but, in a few days, was as bad as ever; there was no taming her by gentle means. We were forced to tie her up like a man, and give her one dozen with the cat-o'-nine-tails, and assure her of a clawing every offence; this alone reduced her to any kind of order....

The first place we stopped was at Santa Cruz, in the island of Teneriffe, for water....

We did not restrain the people on shore from coming on board through the day. The captains and seamen, who were in port at the time, paid us many visits. Mrs. Barnsley bought a cask of wine, and got it on board with the agent's leave....

A TROUBLESOME CARGO

We next stood for St. Jago, accompanied by two slave ships from Santa Cruz to St. Jago, who sailed thus far out of their course for the sake of the ladies. They came on board every day when the weather would permit. ...

We then stood for Rio Janeiro, where we lay eight weeks ... (our) Jewesses made here a good harvest, and the ladies had a constant run of visitors. I had received fifty suits of child bed linen for their use; they were a present from the ladies of England. I here served out twenty suits. Mrs. Barnsley acted as midwife. ...

In crossing the line, we had the best sport I ever witnessed upon the occasion. We had caught a porpoise the day before the ceremony, which we skinned to make a dress for Neptune with the tail stuffed. When he came on deck, he looked like the best representation of a merman I ever saw, painted, with a large swab upon his head for a wig. Not a man in the ship could have known him. One of the convicts fainted, she was so much alarmed at his appearance, and had a miscarriage after. Neptune made the boys confess their amours to him, and I was really astonished at their number. ...

While we lay at the Cape we had a narrow escape from destruction by fire. The carpenter allowed the pitch-pot to boil over upon the deck, and the flames rose in an alarming manner. The shrieks of the women were dreadful, and the confusion they made running about drove every one stupid. I ran to my birth [*sic*], seized a pair of blankets to keep it down until the others drowned it with water. Captain Aitken made me a handsome present for my exertions. ...

At length, almost to our sorrow, we made the land upon the 3rd of June 1790, just one year all but one day from our leaving the river. We landed all our convicts safe. ...

I saw but little of the colony, as my time was fully

occupied in my duties as steward, and any moments I could spare I gave them to Sarah.

The days flew on eagles wings, for we dreaded the hour of separation, which at length arrived. It was not without the aid of the military we were brought on board. I offered to lose my wages, but we were short of hands . . . The captain could not spare a man . . . I thus was forced to leave Sarah, but we exchanged faith; she promised to remain true, and I promised to return when her time expired, and bring her back to England. I wished to have stolen her away, but this was impossible, the convicts were so strictly guarded by the marines . . . With a heavy heart I bade adieu to Port Jackson, resolved to return as soon as I reached England.

Such was the end of a charming cruise, which ended, unlike most cruises in the eighteenth century, with many more passengers than there had been at the beginning. It was not the end of John Nichol's faithful heart.

He was a penniless seaman, separated from his convict lass by a captain who took precautions against desertion with the bayonet. When and if he arrived in England, she would be at the very opposite end of his humble world, and how could a ship's cooper afford a passage back so far as that?

It was the start of an Odyssey which would have bothered Ulysses.

Nichol decided that he would have to return by jumping ships. From ships which were going in the wrong direction, he must desert at convenient ports — convenient for joining other ships which were headed in the general direction of Australia. He had left her his bible with both their names written in it as the only pledge their simple minds could manage. Now he must fulfil the pledge.

China, the Cape, St. Helena, England; a South-Sea whaler in the hope of deserting at Rio; a shipwreck near the Nore; no Indiamen available; the Falkland Islands, the Straights of Magellan, the Horn: always something happened which defeated his plans: the ship turned back or did not call at the expected port or was actually wrecked. Whaling in the South Seas, they fell in with another vessel from which, by a coincidence, he got some news. Sarah had left the colony for Bombay! 'Unconstant woman! Why doubt my faith? Yet dear, and never to be forgotten, I resolved to follow her to India.'

The outlandish names began again. Tambo, Payta, Rio Janeiro, Lisbon, England once more; a visit on foot to Sarah's parents, to see if they had any news; in 1793, a ship for China; Cape of Good Hope — and now he was growing warm — but the China merchant sailed straight across to Java.

At this point Nichol almost gave in. He had spent four years trying to reach his girl, with the slowly saved money for her passage sewn about his body: she had never sent any message to him or to her parents: she had absconded to Bombay — alone? Java was a dangerous port for desertion, unhealthy and foreign. He gave it up. He would stick to his present ship till she got back to England, pay one more visit to Sarah's family, and then, if he heard no more, he would abandon the quest. 1794 found him back at the Downs — and the press-gang caught him. He had fallen into the dreadful hands of the Royal Navy.

John Nichol never did see Sarah Whitelam again.

THE SCANDALMONGER

Instead, he served in *Edgar*, *Goliath*, *Ramilies* and *Ajax*. He fought at Cape St. Vincent, the blockade of Cadiz, Aboukir Bay: at Malta went blind with ophthalmia: was discharged as ship's corporal on the conclusion of peace in 1801. Even then he walked in vain to Lincoln, in case there might be news of his love.

He got himself a little business in Edinburgh with his prize money, married another woman and settled down. But the war flared up again and, being cured of his blindness, he had to abandon his business for fear of being pressed once more. His wife made him do so. He got a job as a quarryman. They grew poorer and poorer, even when peace came.

I never had any children during the seventeen years we lived together. Margaret, during all that time, never gave me a bad word, or made any strife by her temper; but all have their faults. I will not complain ... At her death, which happened four years ago, I was forced to sell all my property, except a small room, in which I live, and a cellar where I do any little work I am so fortunate as to obtain. This I did to pay the expences of her funeral. ...

Somebody paid the old man's passage to London at this stage, that he might apply for the naval pension to which he was entitled, but the world had its bureaucrats even then. His former captain was dead, and, 'when I applied at the Admiralty Office a clerk told me I had been too long of applying'.

He made his way back to Scotland.

I eke out my subsistence in the best manner I can. Coffee made from the raspings of bread (which I obtain from the bakers), twice a day, is my chief diet. A few potatoes, or anything I can obtain with a few

A TROUBLESOME CARGO

pence, constitute my dinner. My only luxury is tobacco, which I have used these forty-five years. To beg I never will submit. Could I have obtained a small pension for my past services, I should then have reached my utmost earthly wish, and the approach of utter helplessness would not haunt me as it at present does in my solitary home. Should I be forced to sell it, all I would obtain could not keep me and pay for lodgings for one year; then I must go to the poor's-house, which God in his mercy forbid. I can look to my death-bed with resignation; but to the poor's-house I cannot look with composure.
I have been a wanderer, and the child of chance, all my days; and now only look for the time when I shall enter my last ship, and be anchored with a green turf upon my breast; and I care not how soon the command is given.

Noble old fellow! One is thankful to say that in the spring of 1822 a kindly citizen of Edinburgh noticed him in the street. He was walking behind a coal cart with a little shovel, hoping to collect the small-coal for his fire, if any fell out. The citizen befriended him, encouraged him to write his memoirs, corrected the spelling, and saw to it that the book was published.

The copy which belongs to the London Library has a quavering inscription on the title page, in rusty, iron-brown ink:

John Nicol Returns Tha[n]ks
for too Guenes
17 Janarey
1823

CHAPTER SIXTEEN

The Butterfly

I HAVE seen young Astley [wrote Horace Walpole with delight, in 1783], when I was in town last, and henceforth shall believe that nothing is impossible, nay, shall wonder if flying is not brought to perfection... How awkward will a dancer be, for the future, that has not consummate grace on a plain firm floor! But, though Mercury did not tread the air with more sovereign agility than the son, it was the father I contemplated with most admiration! What a being, who dared to conceive that he could make horses dance, and that men, women and children might be trained to possess themselves on, over, round the rapidity of two, three, four racehorses, and neither tremble for their necks, nor forget one attitude that is becoming!... A master-genius I can see do anything. Impossibilities are difficulties only to those who want parts.

In short, Horry had been to the circus. 'A master-genius,' he cried, because a young man in spangles and perfect training had balanced on a galloping quadruped.

The veneration for acrobats, which tempts peeresses to follow them in caravans in order to write novels, or paintresses to cover acres of canvas with pictures of ballet-skirts and the behinds of circus horses, may probably be due to an innate desire for perfection. The airy Mercury who balances, and the shining Pegasus who whirls him round the ring, are at the pitch of muscular development. They have been mastering their craft since infancy, with a practice of several hours every morning, and are probably teetotallers who go to bed at ten o'clock. Riding a horse in a circle may not be an important occupation for a lifetime — though some philosophers have thought that one occupation may be as important as another — but the circus people have brought it to perfection. They have devoted their lives to doing something well. They are also living dangerously.

The fascination of acrobats, the lure of singular achievement reached through danger and difficulty with incredible pains, is the interest of a much maligned person, Beau Brummell.

George Bryan Brummell was born in 1778. His grandfather had been an upper servant to Lord Monson; his father had made and married money, and he himself was to inherit some £30,000, in the days when a pound may have had ten times its present value, untaxed. He was sent to Eton, where he was popular. He was there known as 'Buck' Brummell, was never flogged, was good at toasting cheese, and he introduced his first fashion at the school — a gold buckle in the white stock. Prince Florizel, who was sixteen years his senior, noticed him while he was still a schoolboy, and presented him to a cornetcy in his own crack regiment, the Tenth Hussars.

Brummell spent less than a year at Oxford, where he competed for the Newdigate, and was said to have been second for that prize. He then took up his cornetcy and started the extraordinary career which brought him fame. He seems to have been good at making friends, of whom the first was Florizel himself

THE SCANDALMONGER

— the Regent upon whom his success depended. The future King of England used to come and watch him dress. He had a silver spittoon, because 'he could not spit into clay'. It took him about three hours to put his clothes on — which he generally did three times a day — and once he had donned his hat he could not take it off to the ladies, for he would have lost the angle. Florizel would often stay to dinner and to a bottle or two, when the dressing had been finished, and he used to ask the Beau for advice about his own costume. He is said by the poet Moore to have 'blubbered' when told that Brummell did not like the cut of his coat.

Our hero reigned in the fashionable world of London from 1798 to 1816, by which time he had quarrelled with the Prince, then fled to Calais, having been ruined by play and by tailors' bills. He sponged for the rest of his life, except for a brief period as British Consul at Caen. All care of his person went, says the *Dictionary of National Biography*, 'and from carelessness and disease his habits became so loathsome that an attendant could hardly be found for him'. He died in a *maison de charité* in 1840.

Such are the bare bones of the life of a singular person, and of one who might well be given a fair hearing at this distance of time, after the century of contempt to which he has been subjected. The Victorians thought him a fop and a fool, an empty-headed creature who had dawdled through his whole life in affectation. They called him 'an overdressed and finical puppy'. No judgment could have been less accurate. To understand him at all — indeed, to understand why the future King and the whole aristo-

THE BUTTERFLY

cracy went mad about him — we should have to go back to those acrobats of Walpole's.

Brummell's life was like Astley's; it was the strange, sad life which clowns are said to lead, behind the grease-paint. For one thing, he worked. Surely the Victorian idea of a lounging fop must seem ridiculous to anybody who considers his nine-hour toil of dressing? Surely no aimless and effeminate dandy would rub his naked body with a hair-glove every morning, for two hours, before he dressed at all?

The fact was that Brummell, like the people in the circus ring, was doing something well. It did not matter whether it was worth dressing well, any more than it mattered whether it was worth riding bareback in spangles. It was an invention of his own, his hobby if one likes to put it so, and he devoted more thought and more patient effort to its service than has been devoted to stamp-collecting by philatelists, or to any of the other vagaries of the human mind.

When he had finished rubbing and washing his body, which was a handsome one, he used to sit at his silver toilet set. He was shaved, but preferred to control the more important hairs by plucking them with tweezers. He then donned the first shirt of the day, discussed the creation which he intended to attempt with his valet or with Florizel, and set to work. In the mornings it was usually hessians and pantaloons, or tops and buckskins, with a blue coat and a buff waistcoat. Like all serious artists, he was severe. 'No perfumes,' he used to say, 'but very fine linen, plenty of it, and country washing.' He aimed at the most difficult effect, simplicity. His boots were said to be polished with champagne, but they were restrained in pattern. The beauty of the cloth lay in the cut.

Genius, says the quotation, lies in an infinite capacity for taking pains. 'A master-genius', cried Horry, looking at the equestrian act, 'I can see do anything. Impossibilities are difficulties only to those who want parts.' The impossibilities of Brummell were mastered in the cravat. It was twelve inches broad, and had to be accommodated between his chin and his shoulders. He would lie back in his chair, as if at a dentist's, with his chin in the air, and the snow-white material would be wound round the scrubbed throat. By lowering his chin, the twelve inches would be pressed down until they had fitted themselves to the lesser space available. But, if he lowered the chin at once, they might be forced into some unsightly fold. The object was, as it were, to pleat the twelve inches gently, so that they would settle into the five inches, in regular tiers. Consequently the Beau would continue to lie there spreadeagled, lowering his chin by a centimetre at a time, while at the same time making mysterious writhings or wriggles, like a boa-constrictor, until the Absolute had been achieved. The operation was known as 'creasing down'.

Then came the waistcoat and coat, whose moderated colour-scheme had been discussed: and of course the pantaloons, which he was already wearing, looked as if he had been poured into them. The coat collar rose to the top of his head when put on, but it was not folded down like ours. It was straight, like an overcoat collar turned up for rain, and had to be folded by the wearer's fingers until it lay in exactly the right relationship to his ears, and on a level with them.

THE BUTTERFLY

Finally there was the wig and hat, the snuff-box and the clouded cane, and Brummell was ready for his bottle with Florizel, or for a saunter to Watier's.

The effort took place always twice, and sometimes three times a day. He was an early riser like the acrobats, in spite of the toping, in order to get the work begun.

What groom, one may wonder, has taken such trouble with a horse for the show-ring, or worked so hard at it? Like the groom with his brush and curry-comb, or like the painter who primes his own canvases, he began at the bottom. Those fearsome clothes, in which he could not turn his head, were not thrown upon a dirty body by some languid aesthete: they were applied to a naked foundation which had been cleaned for two hours, with water and friction. Nor — and this is perhaps the strangest feature of the story — does Brummell appear to have been a Narcissus. In a period when everybody sat repeatedly for their own portraits, he seldom or never did so. There is no picture of him in the National Portrait Gallery, nor does any appear to be known of there, except for the frontispiece in Jesse's *Life*. There is also a caricature in Gronow's *Reminiscences*, apart from the portrait here reproduced.

Brummell had two physical interests beside his costume. They were his famous bow, which must have been dictated by the cravat, and the way in which he opened a snuff-box; with the finger and thumb of the same hand. He was fond of snuff-boxes, and had a fine collection.

But perhaps it was the spiritual side of his composition which was the interesting one. It is right to say

THE SCANDALMONGER

'composition', for he had composed it, like a picture. He had created it himself, in his own image, and he was not such a fool as to think that it would be enough to have a physical appearance. He was anything but a fool, and he had made himself a spirit as well as a body.

Brummell lived in the age of the duel, and drew the danger of his acrobatics from that fact. To balance the effrontery of his perfect dress, he had invented an effrontery of manner and mind which must have kept him constantly on the edge of disaster. He made a point of being as rude to everybody as he could be. He had brought into fashion the 'cut', the untroubled look straight through the *vis-à-vis*, without recognition, which left the latter shattered. He was as famous for this as he was for his bow or his snuff-boxes, and, when one considers the difference between a cut in the duelling age and a cut today, perhaps there was some ground for the half-fascinated horror which had made it famous.

He did not stop at cutting. 'Bedford,' said he, to the shrinking Duke of that ilk, fingering his Grace's latest tailor-made, 'do you call this *thing* a coat?' 'Ah,' he remarked to a gentleman called Byng, who was nicknamed Poodle behind his back, on meeting him in a curricle with the French dog, 'ah, how d'ye do, Byng? A family vehicle, I see.' 'Madam,' he observed to a miserable female who had invited him to take tea with her, 'you take medicine — you take a walk — you take a liberty. But you *drink* tea.' 'Why, Sir,' he answered, with superb egoism, to an elderly gentleman who was reproaching him for having ruined his son, 'I did all I could for him. I once gave

GEORGE BRUMMELL

him my arm all the way from White's to Brookes'.' 'Some more of that cider,' he ordered from the butler, when dining out and disapproving of the champagne. At another dinner, when the chicken was tough, 'Here, Atons,' to his dog, 'try if you can get your teeth into that, for I'm damned if I can.' 'What could I do, my dear fellar,' he explained to a gentleman who had inquired why he did not marry a certain lady, 'when I actually saw Lady Mary eat cabbage?'

He disliked the practice of eating vegetables, though he sometimes confessed to taking 'one pea'. He used to hunt the fox to a certain extent, but contented himself with riding through a few gates, stating that it was 'a bore to get up so early in the morning only to get one's boots and leathers splashed by galloping farmers'. He was fastidious. What kind of house did the So-and-so's keep, he was asked. 'Don't ask me, my good fellar. You may imagine, when I tell you, that I actually found a cobweb in my pot de chambre!'

The essence of this persistent rudeness, at his peril, was that he was careful to be rude to everybody. He was no respecter of persons, and made it a point of honour to insult the lowest as well as the highest in the land. An unfortunate parvenue called Mrs. Thompson endeavoured to turn him away from a dinner to which she had not invited him, as he knew, but he also knew that he had been invited to a different house by a Mrs. Johnson. Producing the latter's card, he observed: 'Dear me, how very unfortunate. But, you know, Johnson and Thompson — I mean Thompson and Johnson — are so very much alike. Mrs. Johnson-Thompson, I wish you a very good evening.' On another occasion he knocked up a person who was

THE SCANDALMONGER

actually called Snodgrass, at three o'clock in the morning, and inquired: 'Pray, Sir, is your name Snodgrass?' 'Yes, Sir, it is Snodgrass.' 'Snodgrass. Snodgrass. It is a very singular name. Goodbye, Mr. *Snodgrass*.'

Needlessly brutal, perhaps, but he offered the same effronteries as impartially to the future King of England. 'Wales,' he is supposed to have said to the latter after dinner, 'ring the bell.' After the quarrel which ended their friendship, there took place the most superb piece of cold impertinence in English history.

Florizel and he had quarrelled. Florizel was growing fat, and was ashamed. To emphasize the quarrel and to show the world that he had dropped the Beau, the unfortunate Prince attempted to administer the *coup de grâce* in public — using the Beau's own weapon, the 'cut direct'. They met in St. James's Street, according to one version of the story, the Regent walking with an acquaintance and Brummell with Jack Lee. To make the cut as deadly as possible, Florizel stopped to converse with Lee, while looking straight through Brummell. After some conversation, which the Beau bore patiently, the parties separated and passed on. 'Well, Jack,' said Brummell instantly, when there were a few yards between them, loud enough for all to hear, turning round indeed so that the quaking Florizel might hear it clearly, 'Well, Jack, who's your fat friend?'

The strange feature of these insolences was that the aggressor was defenceless. It must have been some trait of masochism which impelled him to throw himself in the world's face for a gauntlet. He was no duellist, could scarcely have aimed a pistol in that monstrous high cravat, depended only on the quickness of his wit for his impunity. This was what made the tight-rope for the acrobatics. On the one hand, if he fought, he was liable to be killed: on the other, if he did not fight, the character of his curious décor would be blasted. He had to find a way of threading the two dangers.

He was challenged twice at least. An officer whose nose had been shot off in the Peninsular War came to demand an explanation, alleging that the Beau had reported him to be a retired hatter. Brummell apologized effusively, adding as the officer was going: 'Yes, it must be a mistake, for now I come to think of it, I never dealt with a hatter without a nose.' The new insult was too complicated for the challenger to disentangle. The seconds of another gentleman menacingly demanded an apology 'in five minutes'. 'Five minutes!' cried Brummell in mock alarm. 'Five seconds — or sooner if you like.' He had saved his skin and his reputation, in both cases, by the tight-rope quirk of wit.

My dear fellar [he explained to a friend, when describing another scare], perhaps you are not aware of the circumstance, but I am not naturally of an heroic turn. Nevertheless, I once had an affair at Chalk Farm, and a dreadful state I was in, I can tell you; never in my life shall I forget the horrors of the previous night! Sleep was out of the question; and I passed it in pacing my room, cursing the cruelly good joke, for which I was on the eve of being torn from Lady —— and Roman punch for ever. The dawn was to me the harbinger of death, not of another day; and yet I almost hailed it with pleasure; but my

THE SCANDALMONGER

second's step upon the stairs soon neutralized the feeling; and the horrid details, which he carefully explained to me, annihilated the little courage that had survived the anxieties of the night. We now left the house, and no accident of any kind, no fortunate upset, occurred on our way to the place of rendezvous; where we arrived, according to my idea, much too soon, a quarter of an hour before the time named.
There was no one on the ground, and each minute seemed an age, as in terror and semi-suffocation, I awaited my opponent's approach. At length the clock of a neighbouring church announced that the hour of appointment had come; how its tones, brought by the wind across the fields, struck upon my heart! I felt like the criminal when he hears the bell of St. Sepulchre's for the last time. We now looked in the direction of town, but there was no appearance of my antagonist; my military friend kindly hinted that clocks and watches varied — a fact I was well aware of, and which I thought he might have spared me the pleasure of hearing him remark upon; but a second is always such a 'd—d good-natured friend'. The next quarter of an hour passed in awful silence, still no one appeared, not even in the horizon; my companion whistled and, confound him! looked much disappointed; the half-hour struck — still no one; the third quarter, and at length the hour. My centurion of the Coldstream now came up, this time in *truth* my friend, and said to me, and I can tell you they were the sweetest accents that ever fell upon my ear: 'Well, George, I think we may go': 'My dear M——,' I replied, 'you have taken a load off my mind, let us go *immediately*!'

Perhaps the instances given may have made him seem little more than a bully and a buffooning poseur; but it was dangerous to make the superficial condemnation. The hard and polished crust was his protection.

THE BUTTERFLY

Brummell, as has been mentioned, competed for the Newdigate Prize. Secretly, under the initial B, he wrote, they say, of all things, nursery rhymes. I can only find part of his best poem, but it is surprisingly charming and apposite as an apology for his attitude. It is not quoted among the others in Jesse's *Life*, but in a small book called *Wits and Beaux of Society*, published by Grace and Philip Wharton in 1860. 'The butterfly' he was said to have written:

> The butterfly was a gentleman,
>   Which nobody can refute.
> He left his lady-love at home,
>   And roamed in a velvet suit.
>
> I *would* [?] be a butterfly,
>   Born in a bower,
> Christened in a tea-pot,
>   And dead in an hour.

He also wrote light letters of some charm, in the same tone as his description of the duel, and, like so many of the thwarted bachelors of the period, for he never married, he adored his dogs. When his beloved Vick came to die, in their exile at Calais, he sent for two doctors. When she was dead, he shut himself in his room for three days and would see nobody. He said that he had lost his only friend.

There seems to be something pathetic and even brave in the lonely aggressor who could not fight, and who wore the incredible cravat as an armour for the heart which prompted nursery rhymes. The pathological case had been born among a species which did not suit with it, but it had managed to impress itself upon the species by its originality, and

THE SCANDALMONGER

by taking pains in the small specialization which it had carved out for itself. The butterfly was a gentleman, in a generation which expected gentlemen to have 'bottom', and the Beau had proved that he had it. He had proved it by his insolence, and by the other recognized way, gambling. At one time he had won £26,000. In the end, of course, he lost it all.

So there came the midnight flight to Calais, after the opera, and the long years of sponging. On the pittance allowed to him by friends, he continued to live to the top of his bent, in debt. 'I found him', said Greville, 'in his old lodging, dressing; some pretty pieces of old furniture in the room, an entire toilet of silver, and a large green macaw perched on the back of a tattered silk chair with faded gilding; full of gaiety, impudence and misery.' He was busy working a tapestry screen, nearly six feet long, about animals, for the Duchess of York. He continued to keep up appearances. Hungry for a dinner, and offered one by some passing tripper, he refused because the hour was unfashionable. 'Your Lordship is very kind, but really I could not *feed* at such an hour.' Florizel passed on a tour, but would not help him. At last he got the job as consul at Caen, only to lose it again at once. With fatal masochism and perversity, he wrote to the Foreign Office stating that the consulship in that town was redundant and a sinecure — which it was. Lord Palmerston grimly abolished the sinecure, without offering other employment. The debts grew more pressing and the contributions from England less helpful. He had to exchange his cravat for a black one, which would not show the dirt. He began to grow slovenly, ruder, unclean and slightly mad. He still kept the love of dogs, receiving it now from the dog of the hotel.

To poor Stop he had always been extremely partial: the grateful animal invariably sat between his feet at the table d'hôte, and was never known to change his position to any other part of the room: if Brummell happened to be absent at the dinner hour, his canine friend would place himself opposite to his empty chair, his head peering beneath the tablecloth, and his earnest gaze directed towards the door. No one could allure him from his post, no fragments would he accept from any hand but that of his now imbecile benefactor; he was the only creature that continued to keep up any social intercourse with him, and his *instinct* . . . may be said to have been superior to the *intellect* of his adopted master — for he was cleanly.

There is a strange Oscar Wilde-like picture of him in a cheap café, being asked to pay his bill for a cup of coffee and answering, 'Oui, Madame, à la pleine lune, à la pleine lune.' Since nobody would visit him any longer, he invented visitors. The table, with cheap tallow candles, would be set for several, and the servant would announce the imaginary nobles as they came. 'The Duchess of Devonshire!' 'Lord Alvanley!' 'Mr. Sheridan!' The ageing Beau received them with his bow, offering them glasses of beer, which he pretended was champagne. He sold the snuff-boxes and the bijoux till there was nothing left. He was sent to prison. He grew quite filthy. The few who still tried to look after him were in despair.

My dear Sir [wrote one of them from Caen in 1838], I have deferred writing for some time, hoping to be able to inform you that I have succeeded in getting Mr. Brummell into one of the public institutions, but

THE SCANDALMONGER

I am sorry to say that I have failed; I have also tried to get him into a private house; but no one will undertake the charge of him in his present state: in fact, it would be totally impossible for me to describe the dreadful situation he is in. For the last two months I have been obliged to pay a person to be with him night and day, and still we cannot keep him *clean*; he now lies upon a straw mattress, which is changed every day. They will not keep him at the hotel, and what to do I know not: I should think that some of his old friends in England would be able to get him into some hospital, where he could be taken care of for the rest of his days. I beg and entreat of you to get something done for him, for it is quite out of the question that he can remain where he is. The clergyman and physician here can bear testimony to the melancholy state of idiotcy he is in.

Yours faithfully,
C. ARMSTRONG

At last, old, dirty, drivelling and penniless, they dragged him away, kicking and screaming, to a poorhouse kept by nuns.

There, in 1840, mad and forgotten, the acrobat who had lost his public died. He had 'dared to conceive', as Walpole put it, an unusual and difficult feat — the maintenance of a perfectly clean person in perfectly clean clothes: he had applied his 'parts' to the impossibility, and had not forgotten 'one attitude that was becoming'; he had proved himself a 'master-genius' by bringing the whole of London to his feet. Nobody who can force the human race to remember him for a hundred years can have been an unimportant person, and it is a singular truth that the poor butterfly of the teapot had more influence on the readers of this book than had the Duke of Wellington. He introduced the trousers which we are wearing as we read. If we consider this fact for a moment, in all its moral ramifications, we may be able to give some weight to a dictum of Lord Byron's, who said that the three greatest men of the new century were Brummell, Napoleon and himself, in that order.

CHAPTER SEVENTEEN

The Queen, the Queen!

A VISIT to the Age of Scandal might end appropriately with some reference to Queen Victoria. Although her uncle the Regent can only be described with some dubiety as the First Gentleman in Europe, there is a strong case for describing his niece as the Last Gentlewoman — as the last efficient champion of an age of autocratic aristocracy. She was born in 1819, during the Regent's lifetime, during the ascendancy of gossip-mongers like Creevey. She was thirty-one when Beau Brummell died, and she fought throughout her life to preserve the kind of culture which she had inherited.

Unfortunately for the reputation of this astonishing lady, her biographers during the first half of the twentieth century have been inclined to take her as a joke. They have condescended to her undoubted foibles, and have identified her with the prudery, the moral disapproval, the wax fruit, aspidistras, plush and woollen bobbles on the curtains of her contemporaries. She has been identified, indeed, with the period which takes its name from her — with what the French call the *époque de mauvais goût*.

But Victoria was far from being a leader of her people. On the contrary, she devoted her energies towards preventing that Gadarene rush of the proletariat which has led to the bureaucracy of the present day. She was by nature a High Tory, what-

THE QUEEN, THE QUEEN!

ever her early label may have been: she did not believe in Votes for Women or in the extension of the franchise: she fought the democratic power of her ministers from start to finish, and she habitually described the liberal Gladstone as 'that wild fanatical old man of seventy-six'. 'And the G.O.M. at eighty-two', she wrote in 1892, 'is a *very alarming lookout.*'

Queen Victoria, moreover, had many of the interests which distinguished the Age of Scandal. In her gay young days, under the tutelage of her beloved Lord Melbourne, she had adored gossip. Nothing had pleased her more, in their long talks after dinner, than to question that wise, amusing old nobleman about the misalliances which he remembered: about Lady Caroline Lamb, Byron and Miss Chaworth, about the Duke of Queensberry and Mlle Fagniani, or about her own disreputable ancestors.

She herself, in those early days, had become rashly involved in the unhappy scandal of Lady Flora Hastings, who was wrongly suspected of being gravid, but died of dropsy instead. It was in her castle of Windsor that Lord Palmerston attempted to ravish a Lady of the Bedchamber. He had been accustomed to sleep with another lady in that particular bedroom, and, said Anson, 'probably from force of habit blundered in'. Nor, indeed, were many of the other noblemen who graced her reign quite so 'Victorian' as the Edwardians would have us suppose.

The Prime Minister, Lord Melbourne [writes Mr. Fulford] was twice cited as a co-respondent, and although both cases collapsed, the public generally would have endorsed his brother's observation, 'no man's luck can go further'. When Lord Hertford's

THE SCANDALMONGER

will was disputed he was revealed not only as a father of a host of bastards but as the lord of a troupe of prostitutes who were the solace of his closing hours in this transitory world. In the same year Lord Chesterfield was sued because, as a trustee, he had agreed to pay £300 a year to an immoral woman who had been the paramour of the beneficiary of the trust. Before this there had been the long-drawn-out action arising from the question of Lord de Ros cheating at cards, and shortly afterwards Lord Frankfort de Montmorency was sent to prison for twelve months for an indecent libel. He sent out a number of printed letters offering to keep husbands 'insensibly asleep' while wives and their lovers were 'amorously engaged in the drawing-room'. He elected to send one of the attractive prospectuses to the vicar of St. Martin-in the-Fields.

Victoria had the 'deportment' of the eighteenth century, which made her the wonderful queen that she was.

At the age of seventy-two,

the Queen danced with Prince Henry [of Battenburg]; light airy steps in the old courtly fashion; no limp or stick but every figure carefully and prettily danced.

SIR ARTHUR PONSONBY

'I am agreeable to see', said the brother of the King of Denmark, 'the Queen dances like a pot.' (He meant top.)

I remember Queen Victoria attending a concert at the Albert Hall in 1887, two months before the Jubilee celebrations. The vast building was packed to the roof, and the Queen received a tremendous ovation. No one who saw it can ever forget how the little old lady advanced to the front of her box and made two

THE QUEEN, THE QUEEN!

very low sweeping curtsies to the right and to the left of her with incomparable dignity and grace, as she smiled through her tears on the audience in acknowledgement of the thunders of applause that greeted her.

LORD FREDERIC HAMILTON

Like Horace Walpole and the rest of them, she was devoted to animals. Her palaces were peppered with statues of them in the grounds or with golden models of them on the tables. She even had a pet human, the insufferable ghillie John Brown, and of him, too, there was a golden model.

Like Walpole, she was a writer of memoirs, publishing two volumes of her own diary and being with difficulty restrained from writing an indiscreet biography of Brown. Incidentally, this supposedly pernickety old lady used always to drink by preference — what does one suppose? Whisky. When Brown was asked whether they took tea on their picnics together, he replied: 'Wall, no, she don't much like tea. We tak oot biscuits and sperruts.'

Like Walpole and the Prince Regent, she was a builder. Balmoral was in some ways the logical Scots baronial development of Strawberry Hill, and the Durbar Room at Osborne was nearly as astonishing as the Pavilion at Brighton. She was musical like George III, and, like him, she was fond of riding, preferring to review her troops on horseback rather than from a carriage. ('Sweet Little Rosy went Beautifully!!') Like George IV, she was a good linguist, and could remember all her clothes and possessions, just as he did. Since she was a millionaire in her own right, whose possessions were on the same scale as her asparagus bed at Frogmore — which was only 2220 yards long — this was a real feat of memory. She had the courage of George II, the distinctive 'bottom' of the eighteenth century, as she proved on the numerous occasions when maniacs tried to assassinate her. Once, on being told that an attempt was likely to be made, she insisted on driving out as usual, but refused to take her lady-in-waiting with her.

Tenacious of etiquette, intransigent about her royal rights, easily moved to tears by public demonstrations of loyalty, pig-headed, brave, kind to old people, young people or poor people, accomplished as a singer and fond of amateur theatricals, artistic enough to try painting and even engraving, incredibly industrious — she is said to have dealt, somehow or other, with 28,000 documents from the Foreign Office alone in 1848 — occasionally ridiculous like all her ancestors from Hanover, this prodigious old Tory gathered into her own reactionary character nearly all the traits of Walpole's period. She was a survival, not a pioneer.

The clue to Queen Victoria's nature, which everybody seems to overlook, was that she was an only child.

The Queen has no hesitation in saying that she was quite devoted to dolls & played with them till she was 14. Her favourites were small ones & small wooden ones which c^d. be dressed as she liked & had a House. None of her children loved them as she did — but then *she* was an *only* child & except occasional visits of other children lived always *alone*, without companions. Once a week one child [Miss Victoria ... Mrs. Harrison] came & occasionally other [? young cousins] came [. . .] but the Queen *really* LIVED alone *as a child.*

Queen's partly illegible Minute

THE QUEEN, THE QUEEN!

It was this loneliness of up-bringing which explained her aristocratic philosophy of Individualism. If she had not been a Tory, she would have been an anarchist — never a socialist: for to her the word 'democrat' was a term of abuse. Sir C. Dilke, she said furiously, was 'a democrat — a disguised Republican'.

It also explains her genuine passion and pathetic mourning for the Prince Consort. He had been the one person with whom this fundamentally lonely woman could cease to be alone. No wonder, with this great opportunity for companionship before her, that her hand had trembled so much that she could scarcely hold the paper from which she read to the Privy Council the announcement of her engagement. ('He is so good and kind, and loves me for myself.') No wonder, when he was dead, that there was ever afterward a picture of him and a wreath, attached to his pillow on the double bed.

Only-children are generally of strong character and often of penetrating intelligence. It accounted for her self-will and for her almost frightening sincerity. Few parents have been willing and able to admit that they do not love their own children. Queen Victoria, who adored babies and was loved by her grandchildren, was able to write to the Queen of Prussia with spartan truthfulness:

Balmoral,
Oct. 6, 1856

... I see the children much less & even here, where Albert is often away all day long, I find no especial pleasure or compensation in the company of the elder children. You will remember that I told you this at Osborne. Usually they go out with me in the afternoon (Vicky mostly, & the others also sometimes), or occasionally in the mornings when I walk or ride, accompanied by my lady-in-waiting, & only very occasionally do I find the rather intimate intercourse with them either agreeable or easy. You will not understand this, but it is caused by various factors. Firstly, I only feel properly *à mon aise* & quite happy when Albert is with me; secondly, I am used to carrying on my many affairs quite alone; & then I have grown up all alone, accustomed to the society of adult (& never with younger) people — lastly, I cannot get used to the fact that Vicky is almost grown up. To me she still seems the same child, who had to be kept in order & therefore must not become too intimate. Here are my sincere feelings in contrast to yours.

Her decisiveness, capriciousness, dignity, inconsiderateness, charm and friendliness, obstinacy, imperiousness, intolerance of opposition, good sense and self-confidence: all were typical of the only child.

'We are not amused' is probably the old Queen's most famous remark. It is salutary to reflect that her journal generally says exactly the opposite.
We came home at ¼ to 12. I was VERY MUCH AMUSED INDEED ! ! !

April 26th, 1834

She was often a Tartar, one has to admit, but it was odd how an almost raffish humour kept breaking through. At Balmoral she once organized a sweepstake on the Derby! This was during the years of her deepest retirement — years which largely remained a mystery to Lytton Strachey, but which have become clearer since the publication of the *Life* of Sir Henry Ponsonby, her private secretary. Some of Ponsonby's notes are far from melancholy.

THE QUEEN, THE QUEEN!

One evening Prince John of Glücksburg, whose English was not perfect, heard from a lady, who came down late and sat next to him, that she had locked her door and could not open it for some time. He repeated this loudly across the table: 'So you see she was confined before dinner.'

Did you ever hear of Lady Tatton telling her coachman to look at a horse she wanted to buy — and he advised her not to buy it. She said 'Why? What part of him is bad?' The coachman replied, 'Why, My Lady, I don't like 'is 'ocks nor 'is ass nor anything that is 'is.'

I do not know why my remarks are supposed always to be facetious when they are not. I simply asked what the tourists thought of their relationship. [Dr. Jenner and the German governess had climbed a mountain.] He replied 'Oh, of course they thought she was Madame,' which created some laughter. Then he added, 'The guide was very decided and made us give up the horses we rode up and come down in a chair.' 'What?' I asked. 'Both in one chair?' Well, there is nothing odd in this — but everyone laughed. I turned to Mary Bids [Lady Biddulph]. She was purple. On the other side I tried to speak to Princess Louise. She was choking. I looked across to Jenner. He was convulsed. Of course this was too much. I gave way; and we all had a *fou rire* till the tears ran down my cheeks which set off the Queen. I never saw her laugh so much. She said afterwards it was my face. At last we got a pause when Jane [Lady Churchill] to set things straight again began with 'Did you find it comfortable?' which started us off again. My laugh was at Jenner stuffing his napkin over his mouth to stop himself, at Mary Bids shaking and speechless at my side, and at Bids' solemn face.

Yesterday the Queen was on the rampage....

THE SCANDALMONGER

I didn't get back [to the ball] till 11.30 when I found some asperity at my absence. Explanations ensued, culminating in my dancing a Hooligan [reel] with the Queen.

Sir Henry Ponsonby must have been one of the nicest people at Victoria's court, and future historians may find that he was one of the more important. In her youth, the Queen had suffered a 'pash' for Lord Melbourne; in her middle years, she had adored the Prince Consort; and in her old age the humbug Disraeli managed to twist her round his finger with most of the arts of the gigolo. From 1870 to 1895, Ponsonby stood patiently in the shadow behind the throne, shunning all notice, absorbing all shocks, listening to everybody, toning down the royal tantrums, smoothing the rows, pacifying the raging ministers, maintaining the peace of Europe, bowing his head to the storms and smiling with his own delicious sense of humour. He was one of the silent humorists.

(Correspondence about Court dress at a function)
Minister in Attendance to H.M. Private Secretary.
Dear Ponsonby,
    Is it 'knees'?
                                            Yrs. W.V.H.

Private Secretary to Minister in Attendance
Dear Harcourt,
    As no ladies will be present, trousers will be worn.
                                            Yrs. H.F.P.

A big, untidy man with a melancholy beard, generally turning up with his trousers too long or wearing two of the same medal, absolutely unimpressed by titles and unafraid of the Queen whom he loved, served,

THE QUEEN, THE QUEEN!

understood and managed, her secretary had two kinds of laugh. His diplomatic laugh was loud and hearty; his private laugh, the one he genuinely used over the incident of the German governess, was silent. He would just go scarlet in the face, shake all over, and the tears would trickle down his cheeks. (This was as well for him, since the Queen disapproved of loud laughter.)

He managed her superbly.

When she insists that 2 and 2 make 5 I say that I cannot help thinking they make 4. She replies there may be some truth in what I say, but she knows they make 5. Thereupon I drop the discussion. It is of no consequence and I leave it there, knowing the fact. But X— goes on with it, brings proofs, arguments and former sayings of her own. No one likes this. No one can stand admitting they are wrong, women especially; and the Queen can't abide it. Consequently she won't give in, says X— is unkind and there is trouble.

The Queen asked me who could represent her [at the funeral of the Empress of Russia]. I said, the Duke of Edinburgh. The Queen said 'No, of course he couldn't.' I said 'Of course he couldn't.' But as I did not know why, I got back to him in the course of conversation and said it was a pity he couldn't. So she telegraphed to ask him if he could and he said he would.

Such was the character of perhaps the last monarch who seriously tried to maintain the ideals and civilization of the Age of Scandal. It will be remembered from what has been shown in the first volume that her ancestors had always combined a fairly high level of culture with a flair for the absurd. Indeed, if one were compelled to define the earlier period in two words,

THE SCANDALMONGER

one might suggest that Horace Walpole's era combined the sublime with the ridiculous. So did the Queen. She was ridiculously like the two chess queens in Lewis Carroll, mixed with the Duchess and the Queen of Hearts. She was sublime enough to become the first English sovereign with the title of Empress. One of the best illustrated books of the Age of Scandal had been the *Microcosm of London*. In it, the sublime Pugin drew the elegant architecture, while the ridiculous Rowlandson added the human figures. So with the Queen. Perhaps we may leave her on that note — the terrible old individualist and champion of earlier elegancies driving before her a rout of Rowlandson descendants — with a final quotation from Sir Henry Ponsonby:

Yesterday Haig and I went out towards the garden by the side door when we were suddenly nearly carried away by a stampede of Royalties, headed by the Duke of Cambridge and brought up by Leopold, going as fast as they could. We thought it was a mad bull. But they cried out, 'The Queen, the Queen,' and we all dashed into the house again and waited behind the door till the road was clear.

Well, the road is clear now and they are all safely past. All the fantastic kings and noblemen of the age which we have been discussing have given way before the demonstrably false proposition of Washington, that all men are born equal. They are not. Dr. Johnson was born with scrofula, while Sixteen-string Jack the highwayman was born with a perfect body; Selwyn was born a fool, while Porson came into the world with the brain of a great scholar. I for one am sorry to see the old distinctions go. I would rather have lived at a time when the private enterprise of a great Duke could produce the lovely palace of Stowe with all its graces, rather than now, when an omnipotent proletariat can rear a block of offices to house the redundant inspectors and the forms in triplicate of the T.U.C.

NOTES ON THE ILLUSTRATIONS

BLOODY NEWS attributed to Gillray but stated by Mrs. George to be by Ansell. On the gallows is written 'Late Abershaw'. Tierney, under the gallows, exclaims: 'D— it. One might as well shoot at a rush light.' (Pitt was thin.) His second says: 'Oh what a Pity 'tis, it did not hit his waistcoat.' The British Lion rolls on its back in agitation, crying: 'Oh dear! oh dear!' Britannia swoons with: 'Oh Murder! my Darling's in Danger, oh! oh!' Dundas, Pitt's second, reassures her: 'Never fear, your favourite Boy is in no Danger, if I was as well made for fighting, I'd challenge them all.' Pitt delopes. This particular duel was fought on Putney Heath, where a famous highwayman named Abershaw had been hanged for shooting a constable. The gallows seems to point a similarity between Tierney and the highwayman. As a matter of fact, Abershaw was quite a nice highwayman; for he spent his last days drawing pictures of his exploits on the cell walls with cherry juice, and rode to his death with a rose in his mouth. The Pitt-Tierney duel was fought because Pitt had been rude to Tierney in parliament. Both men fired twice, but neither was hit. A large crowd was present, including the Speaker of the House of Commons!

Lord Camelford. This engraving appeared in Kirby's *Wonderful Museum*, 1805; but the copy of the book at the British Museum was destroyed during the war.

Illustration from Tyburn Chronicle, IV 309. The illustration is an original indian ink wash (with pen outlines) by S. Wale, R.A. This illustration, and others, appeared in the *Tyburn Chronicle*, but there they appeared in reverse (as they were engraved). S. Wale was an illustrator (and painter), and a pupil of Hayman. He worked in London chiefly as an illustrator of books (particularly the *Tyburn Chronicle* and the *Newgate Calendar*). He was the first professor of perspective at the Royal Academy. Born 1720 (?), he died in 1786. The actual illustration is of the execution of Jacobite Rebels

NOTES ON THE ILLUSTRATIONS

on Kensington Common, 1746. Notice that the rebels are wearing tartans. The executioner is showing the head of the naked corpse to the spectators.

Rural Scene by Rowlandson. This is usually called 'The Haymakers'. In 1787, says Grego, 'Rowlandson issued a series of rustic sketches including such subjects as horses, dogs, coaches, carts, haymakers, cottages, farrier's forges and roadside inns; similar views to those selected by Morland but treated in Rowlandson's own original style.'

Old Q on the Balcony. Nothing is known of the source of the engraving. The British Museum describe it as anonymous, and no other works of reference mention it.

Chevalier d'Eon. This appears in the *London Magazine* for September 1777, where it is described as 'a striking likeness of Mad. de Beaumont, commonly called the Chevalier d'Eon ... neatly engraved'. It accompanies an article entitled 'Memoirs of Mademoiselle d'Eon' and the article contains the following reference to the engraving: '... in order to convey a proper idea of the person of this lady, in whom we shall find a strange heterogeneous compound of male and female qualities, we obtained a striking resemblance of her face, from an original drawing from life, by a private gentleman, at the time of the disputes between d'Eon and the Count de Guercy'.

Scene in Bedlam by Hogarth. This is the eighth plate of *The Rake's Progress.* The Rake is in front, finally mad, with his faithful female friend, doctor and warden. Apart from the two lady visitors, the eccentrics include, from left to right, a religious maniac, an astronomer, a mathematician discovering the longitude, a royal claimant, a tailor, a musician, a despised lover and a person who believes himself to be the Pope. The lover has scratched on the banisters 'charming Betty Careless'.

Chairing the Member by Hogarth. Inscription: 'We must' (on the sun-) dial (die all). 'In Le Brun's Battle of the Granicus, an eagle is represented as hovering over the plumed helmet of Alexander; this thought is very happily

THE SCANDALMONGER

parodied in a goose, flying immediately over the tie-wig of our exalted candidate.' The nobleman in a ribbon in the background is said to be the Duke of Newcastle.

Uncorking Old Sherry by Gillray. '— the honble Gent.' tho' he does not very often addreſs the House, yet when he does, he always thinks proper to pay off all arrears, & like a Bottle just uncork'd bursts all at once, into an explosion of Froth & Air; — then, whatever might for a length of time lie lurking & corked up in his mind, whatever he thinks of himself or hears in conversation — whatever he takes many days or weeks to sleep upon, the whole common place book of the interval is sure to burst out at once, stored with studied Jokes, Sarcasms, arguments, invectives, & every thing else, which his mind or memory are capable of embracing whether they have any relation or not to the Subject under discuſsion — See Mr. P-tts speech on y^r Gen^t Defence Bill. March 6th 1805. Sheridan is in the bottle: Pitt is uncorking him: Fox is in the third bottle from the right.

Tales of Wonder by Gillray. The book on the table is *The Monk*, by Lewis. Note the ornaments and the painting.

Ci-devant Occupations by Gillray. On the table before Barras lies General Buonaparte's military commission. The caption reads: 'ci-devant Occupations — or — Madame Talian and the Empress Josephine dancing Naked before Barrass in the Winter of 1797 — a Fact! — Barrass (then in Power) being tired of Josephine, promised Buonaparte a promotion, on condition that he would take her off his hands: Barrass had, as usual, drank freely & placed Buonaparte behind a Screen, while he amused himself with these two Ladies, who were then his humble dependants — Madame Talian is a beautiful Woman, tall & elegant: Josephine is smaller and thin, with bad Teeth something like Cloves — it is needless to add that Buonaparte accepted the Promotion & the Lady — now, Empress of France!' Judging by the teeth, Josephine is the lady nearer to Napoleon in this piece of eighteenth-century propaganda.

NOTES ON THE ILLUSTRATIONS

George Brummell Esq. See the author's remarks on p. 197. First the known portraits are:

(1) The painting of the 'Children of William Brummell Esq.' by Sir Joshua Reynolds, which my informant, Mr. Conan Nicholas, has seen at Ken Wood House. This shows George Brummell as a child of five or six with his elder brother.

(2) The caricature in Gronow's *Reminiscences*.

(3) The frontispiece to Jesse's *Life*, 1844 edition. But in the later edition, 1885 I think, there is a different frontispiece, which is I believe an illustrator's idea of Brummel, i.e. contemporary to 1885. In this edition the frontispiece to vol. I of the 1844 edition appears in colour about half way through vol. II.

(4) The portrait in this book.

(5) A lithograph signed 'D.C.W. 1838'. This is in the British Museum but is not catalogued. It is reproduced in a recent volume on Brummell where the authoress says 'sometimes attributed to Wilkie'. The latter attribution is to the mind of Mr. Conan Nicholas nonsensical. It is not, he says, in Wilkie's manner; in any case he was Sir David Wilkie and never David C. Wilkie; and finally the lithograph seems to have been done when Brummel was at Caen.

To return to our portrait. This first appeared in *Bentley's Miscellany* in 1844. Here it is described as 'engraved from a miniature, by J. Cook'. The British Museum catalogue of portraits says that the artist is unknown, and gives the engraver as J. Cook. *Bentley's Miscellany* also says in a footnote that the portrait of George Brummell is 'from an original miniature'. And the note continues: 'We are indebted to Mr. John Hooper of Sevenoaks for this interesting miniature' and goes on to say that he has a marvellous collection which he would be glad to show anyone who cared to visit his house at Sevenoaks. Jesse says that when Brummell died, his trunk contained only several packets of letters, a few silver spoons, etc., and a miniature. Could this have been the miniature that eventually came into Mr. John Hooper's possession?